*Essays & Studies 1983*

# Essays & Studies 1983

Collected by
## Beatrice White

HUMANITIES PRESS
Atlantic Highlands, N.J.

ESSAYS AND STUDIES 1983
IS VOLUME THIRTY-SIX IN THE NEW SERIES
OF ESSAYS AND STUDIES COLLECTED ON BEHALF OF
THE ENGLISH ASSOCIATION

Typeset by Inforum Ltd, Portsmouth
Printed by The Pitman Press

ISBN 0–391–02834–0

# *Preface*

The collector of this volume of *Essays and Studies* wishes to express her deep gratitude to the contributors who each came to the aid of the Association in a critical emergency. Without the active and courageous co-operation of these seven people, it would have been impossible to assemble the volume in the time available.

Beatrice White
Emeritus Professor of English
Language and Literature
University of London

# Contents

# I

## Yorick's Place in 'Hamlet'[1]

### ELIZABETH MASLEN

For nearly two hundred years (since the graveyard scene, cut by
Garrick towards the end of his career, was restored to performance),
Yorick's function in the popular view of *Hamlet* has been as an object
in the prince's hand, the focal point of his melancholy. Hamlet with
the skull has been used by a long succession of artists as a visual
image central to the play. To mention only a few examples, there
was an *Illustrated London News* portrayal of Macready in 1846, head
jetting funeral plumes, morosely addressing Horatio over the skull;
there was Sandor Jaray's sculpture at the turn of the century, where
Hamlet leans against a draped tombstone, head bent pensively and
privately over the skull; while London Transport's *Theatre London*
(1980) has on its front cover Ken Cox's flamboyant variation on the
same theme. So the skull in Hamlet's hand has become a symbol of
latterday melancholy, visually linked to the skulls of Romantic
Gothick tradition. And while full scholarly cognizance has been
given to the difference between Romantic and Renaissance notions
of melancholy, the skull in *Hamlet* appears to retain its post-Romantic
associations which obscure, I would suggest, Yorick's true function
in the play.

There is a touch of irony here; for while visual artists have tended
to stress the importance of the skull, Yorick, of all Shakespeare's
fools, seems to have attracted the least scholarly and critical attention. Certainly Enid Welsford in her classic work ignores him[2], as
does Robert Goldsmith[3]. However, William Willeford[4] gives him

---

[1] All references for the text of *Hamlet* are taken from the New Arden
edition, edited by Professor Harold Jenkins (Methuen, 1982). As a former
student of his, I can only record my sense of presumption in writing on a play
in the wake of so fine a scholar and teacher.
[2] Enid Welsford, *The Fool, His Social and Literary History* (Faber and Faber
Ltd, 1935).
[3] Robert H. Goldsmith, *Wise Fools in Shakespeare* (Liverpool University
Press, 1974).
[4] William Willeford, *The Fool and His Scepter* (Northwestern University
Press, 1969).

some emphasis. Much of his argument concerning *Hamlet* is a psycho-analytical development of Dr Johnson's widely accepted view of Hamlet's own resemblance to the Shakespearian fool (and, by exten-sion, of Coleridge's suggestion that the fool's role is disseminated throughout the play). But Dr Willeford also sees Yorick's skull as 'a lodestone to which [Hamlet] is drawn throughout the action, while intending instead to earn his right to his father's throne'. He continues:

> The death's head and skeleton are traditional emblems of the fool in the sense that death makes a fool of life's joys and purposes, as may be seen in graphic representations by Dürer, Holbein, and others. And even more in keeping with the fundamental action of the play, the hero-prince's familiarity with the cynical Grave-digger as they contemplate the skull of the jester is a final epiph-any, outside the course of consequential events, of the disinte-gration of the social structure, the death of the body politic that now can only await renewal from without.

He sees Yorick's skull as 'an emblem of Hamlet's folly', while also asserting: 'the fact that the skull is unearthed in the grave intended for [Ophelia] implies a relation between the jester and the girl as factors in Hamlet's fate.' And he concludes: 'In Yorick's skull, too, the force is at last objectified that has blocked Hamlet from assuming his father's throne and marrying his destined bride.'

Much of Dr Willeford's reading of the evidence seems over-interpretative. But the objection that concerns me here is that, as in the case of most of the artists and critics just mentioned, Yorick's function is analysed mainly in terms of Hamlet himself. My conten-tion is that Yorick as skull is playing a crucial role in *Hamlet*, and not in relation to Hamlet alone: his skull is of considerable structural importance to the idea of the play. In Shakespeare's practice, accord-ing to the mainstream of criticism, the fool acts pre-eminently as a balancing factor, counteracting in some measure extremes of word or action in his patrons. Such is his role in *As You Like It*, *Twelfth Night*, and *King Lear*. And Yorick, while being dead, has not aban-doned this function of the fool.

For in *Hamlet*, there are two visitants from beyond the grave, each introduced at carefully pointed moments of the play's development: the ghost of the king who walks unnaturally and unquietly, and the skull of his jester, also wrenched from rest, but the emblem of natural mortality. While the Ghost tempts men 'With thoughts beyond the reaches of our souls' (I.iv.56), Yorick plays the earthbound *memento mori*, a reminder of death the leveller. And, as I hope to show, the neatness of counterpointing King's Ghost and Fool's skull is not an oversimplification of a vastly complex play, but central to its dramatic structure. I shall begin then with the Ghost, which does not 'frame' the action like Andrea's Ghost in Kyd's *Spanish Tragedy*, but dominates the initial stages of the play.

Unlike the later *Macbeth, Hamlet* does not start by confronting audience alone with the supernatural. Instead, the Ghost appears to the watch and to the sceptical man of reason, Horatio. When it appears, as Professor Jenkins stresses, Shakespeare reveals its dramatic function gradually, maintaining throughout an ambivalence as to its spiritual status. Yet Horatio is at once convinced by the evidence of his own eyes; and what he sees (according to his own words), together with how he interprets what he sees, guides the audience's first response. The Ghost is 'like the King', but in a particular guise: it assumes 'that fair and warlike form/ In which the majesty of buried Denmark/ Did sometimes march' (I.i.50–2). Nor is it simply armed: 'Such was the very armour he had on/ When he th' ambitious Norway combated' (I.i.63–4). Marcellus confirms this 'martial' impression and asks a question linking the Ghost from the past with the warlike preparations of the present. Horatio's reply performs a similar function, linking the present dangers of 'young Fortinbras' directly with 'th'ambitious Norway' whom the particular armour of the Ghost recalls. At this point, the interpretation of the Ghost's appearances seems clear: it is in the public role of King, rather than in the private role of man that we are invited to see him. Yet even here there is a certain irony: concern for Denmark may be the reason for the Ghost's 'martial stalk', yet he was prepared to gamble the whole or part of that realm on single combat with old Fortinbras; and in both the earlier *I Henry IV* and the later *King Lear*, Shakespeare connects rashness with easy readiness to split kingdoms. 'Our valiant Hamlet' (I.i.87) may have been a bold spirit of an heroic age but, as has frequently been remarked, his boldness does not belong to Renaissance notions of kingship and would be as alien to Shakespeare's audience as his awesome ghostly walkings. Certainly his interpretation of kingship, according to Horatio's report, might be seen to need, like Lear's, the balancing influence of a Fool.

The Ghost's second appearance increases the effect of apartness. Here, the dialogue of Horatio and his companions concentrates more on the habits of ghosts than on the state of Denmark. 'Extorted

treasure' is added to its possible reasons for walking, while super-
stitions concerning ghosts overshadow its kingly function as portent
of its 'country's fate'. Its otherness from the world of men predominates, for however Horatio and the watch may debate its source
and significance, it fails to speak. Yet this ghost, this 'shape' of a
bygone age, is expected to communicate with the world of men, and
'young Hamlet' is named as the most likely person to break its
silence.

So the first scene leaves us with vivid theatrical impressions of
conflict and doubt: the Ghost is as alien and awesome a figure as the
knightly image stretched out on its tomb in church, then as now its
emblems betokening warlike prowess, its motives as obscure as the
tomb itself. There is precious little of *memento mori* in such images *per
se*: they stress earthly achievement alone and serve only to emphasize
the unearthliness of the Ghost's unease. In some mediaeval and
Renaissance visual art, a *memento mori* was indeed often introduced,
and this tendency (which underwent considerable regeneration in
the late sixteenth and early seventeenth centuries) is certainly
germane to *Hamlet*, as I hope to show.

The movement from the Ghost to Claudius holding court is, at
first, extreme. Here is a king who can set the 'delight and dole' of a
brother's death and a hasty marriage in the context of reasons of
state; and the use of the royal plural, the proper acknowledgement of
'your better wisdoms', and the confident handling of the 'young
Fortinbras' problem may serve to convince us that this is the right
king for the moment. His handling of Laertes, too, where the language becomes more intimate, 'you' and 'your' quickly giving way to
'thou' and 'thine', appears to promise well for the man as for the
King.

Yet visually this is not all. Against the loquacious briskness of the
scene is set a silent figure in 'nighted colour', 'inky cloak', who is
unnamed until line sixty-three. The Ghost was in armour, this man
apart in mourning at a time of apparent national crisis. However
ambivalent the Ghost may have seemed, the emphasis laid in the first
scene on Fortinbras must surely link it with Claudius's apparent
concerns as well as with Hamlet's apartness. The audience must
remain victim of confusion in the light of what follows. Young
Hamlet, as has been amply illustrated by critics, is typical of the
Melancholy man of the Renaissance, yet Shakespeare as ever uses
commonplace to revitalize the idea. For as King and Queen turn to
Hamlet, they offer him *memento mori* consolation for the death of his

father, persisting for some forty lines, and he refuses this consolation. Here the audience is offered double vision of considerable
irony. Young Hamlet, at a time of seeming public danger, appears
determinedly obsessed with private grief, which must make him
seem irresponsible. But at the same time, the audience knows that
the consolation offered here is challenged by the very existence of the
Ghost. Hamlet is also linked with Wittenberg, surely for playgoers,
at this moment of double vision, recalling more aptly the perilous
supernatural associations of Faustus than the reforming zeal of
Luther. And Hamlet's first soliloquy then follows (I.ii.129).

The placing of this piece of self-revelation is masterly. We are
shown why Hamlet is in no state to accept *memento mori* consolation:
the naturalness of death is obscured for him by an unnatural view of
the world, and he has been offered the consolations of nature by the
two people he sees as behaving most unnaturally. Moreover, his
images for his father are revealing: they stress myth and legend as
inevitably associated with old Hamlet. So here he is Hyperion to
Claudius's satyr, and Claudius may be 'My father's brother—but no
more like my father/ Than I to Hercules' (I.ii.152–3). Hamlet's
alienation is extreme: from life (and so from natural consolations for
death); from natural affection and kinship (by Gertrude's 'frailty' and
Claudius's unworthiness). And far from introducing anything
that may help this dangerous state of mind, Shakespeare brings on
Horatio (ironically, as sceptic and scholar, the one character to date
who might offset the balance) with his unnatural news.

It seems to me important that, while the audience knows from his
soliloquy the full extent of Hamlet's melancholy disorientation,
Horatio is kept in ignorance of it for the time being. For Horatio and
audience, the comment: 'My father—methinks I see my father' holds
irony, but of different kinds. The audience, unlike Horatio, knows
that Hamlet is haunted by obsessions of melancholy; deploring the
unnaturalness of his natural world he is seeking with 'vailed lids'
inflated images of his 'noble father in the dust' (I.ii.70–1). To bring
a conjunction between the supernatural and these melancholic
promptings must be explosive; and, with supremely handled irony,
Horatio is given no chance by the play to assess Hamlet's mood
before the prince meets the Ghost. All Hamlet's conversation, both
in the questioning about the apparition and as they await its next
appearance, is that of a rational man meeting a shocking emergency
and of a crisply cynical commentator on the state of Denmark.
Furthermore, when the explosion occurs, Horatio is in no position to

offer *memento mori* advice, since the play has taken care to have him
convinced of the Ghost's actuality.

When Hamlet meets the Ghost, it is still in a public context: the
state of Denmark has just been discussed. However, after his initial
defensive prayer and comment on the dubious origins of ghosts, he is
quick to address it as his father; the 'mind's eye' and the evidence of
his senses have converged. But he reminds us, by his evocative
recollection of the tomb (I.iv.46–51), that this ghost has broken the
bonds of *memento mori*; and he acknowledges the perils of this breach
of the natural laws of death when he asks why the apparition comes
'So horridly to shake our disposition/ With thoughts beyond
the reaches of our souls' (I.iv.55–6). Like the later Macbeth then,
although in a very different frame of mind, he knows precisely
where the visitation may lead him: beyond the bounds of what
reasonable natural order may contain or control. And Horatio's
warning echoes this awareness when he asks, what if it 'might
deprive your sovereignty of reason/ And draw you into madness'
(I.iv.73–4). The play has already shown Hamlet's loss of confidence
in the natural order. In Hamlet's case, as in Macbeth's, the supernatural will merge and give authority to material already in
the mind, as Horatio discovers too late: 'He waxes desperate with
imagination' (I.iv.87). But unlike Macbeth or Faustus, Hamlet never
dallies with the supernatural. He has it thrust upon him, and in a
form hard to resist: the Ghost of a loved and admired father.

As the Ghost speaks, Hamlet's dangerous vulnerability is obvious.
For after portentous hints of purgatory, it reveals a purpose far
removed from the threat of Fortinbras and the public concerns of
Kingship. Its plea for vengeance is strictly personal, merging so aptly
with Hamlet's earlier broodings that it has too often removed
Hamlet from the theatre to the psychiatrist's couch. In terms of the
play, however, we might note that this ghost, again like the armed
figure on a church tomb, may represent all things to all men: for
Horatio and the watch it is the public King, warning of national
danger or extorted treasure; for Hamlet it is a murdered brother and
wronged husband. The play will come full circle: brother and
husband are avenged within the action, Fortinbras will acquire what
'our valiant Hamlet' retained and took with more recklessness than
responsibility. But within the circle of this dance of death, Yorick
will eventually play a traditional and crucial part.

The Ghost has indeed posed a complex of problems. Is it old
Hamlet or masquerading as old Hamlet? Is it from heaven or hell? Is

the reason for its hauntings public, private, or both? Audience and characters within the play will judge by their own premise; and this method of judging, without a common yardstick, will inform the greater part of the action. For each character sees others according to his own lights: thus, Polonius sees Hamlet as lovelorn, while Gertrude sees him as distracted by the 'o'er hasty marriage'. Claudius's view is veiled by a show of public and private concern until the revealing aside: 'The harlot's cheek, beautied with plast'ring art,/ Is not more ugly to the thing that helps it/ Than is my deed to my most painted word' (III.i.51–3). Rosencrantz and Guildenstern, royally summoned, soon reveal that friendship is coloured by sub-servience to Claudius. All interpret Hamlet's and each other's actions by the natural or unnatural actions of which they are aware in their own finite worlds. But Hamlet's melancholy, prompted initially by worlds they recognize, has had the further stimulus which came 'So horridly to shake our disposition/ With thoughts beyond the reaches of our souls'. In the worlds of the court, while he may play the role of fool to several other characters, be it according to an 'antic dis-position' or the insights of madness, the theatre audience alone sees this. Those teased and goaded by him cannot profit from his 'fooling', as each has cast him in a role of their own devising. Furthermore, he can neither play the all-important role of fool for himself, nor trust another sufficiently for that role. Even Horatio can give him love but no philosophy, since all human wisdom is rendered ineffectual by Hamlet's predisposition to melancholy and his uneasy contract with a ghost. The play lends him no yardstick by which he can measure those 'thoughts beyond the reaches of our souls', however he may debate them. 'Your philosophy' is therefore rejected as a science of the natural world by a man debarred from nature through his overwhelming experience of the unnatural and supernatural (cf II.ii.295–310). Hamlet is more at home in the players' fantasy world and, while he sees it for what it is in his soliloquy (II.ii.544–601), he chooses to bend this illusory art to his purpose. The peril he stands in, the peril Horatio saw too late (I.iv.87), emerges most clearly after the play-within-the-play when he once again 'waxes desperate with imagination'.

At 'the very witching hour of night', he strives between 'Now could I drink hot blood' and 'Let me be cruel, not unnatural'. His language points to three factions battling within him, the natural, the unnatural, and the supernatural; and in this context the play presents the prayer scene. Here the convention is used of the revenger wishing to damn as well as kill, but again convention is revitalized. The audience hears Claudius's confession; Hamlet sees him at prayer and proceeds to judge him according to the Ghost's prompting and the implicit evidence of the play-within-the-play. For the audience, his desire for Claudius's damnation must recall the Ghost's hints of purgatory, while for Hamlet mere killing becomes means not end; and this leads on to the double standard concerning killing which becomes explicit in the closet scene.

For whereas Hamlet sticks to his resolve to 'speak daggers' to Gertrude, he kills Polonius blindly, on impulse. Yet the discovery of his mistake does not give him pause. This 'rash and bloody deed' is viewed relatively: 'Almost as bad . . ./As kill a king and marry with his brother' (III.iv.28–9). Even allowing for rank, the tone of Polonius's first brief epitaph ('Thou wretched, rash, intruding fool, farewell./ I took thee for thy better' III.iv.31–2), though it may relate the mistake to Claudius, contrasts markedly with what follows: 'Heaven's face does glow/ O'er this solidity and compound mass/ With tristful visage, as against the doom,/ Is thought-sick at the act' (III.iv.48–51). Polonius's body remains on stage, but Hamlet uses this high style for old Hamlet's murder. The father again evokes godlike images; 'Rebellious hell' presides over his mother's sensuality; Claudius is a 'mildew'd ear'.

And crucial to the structure of the play is the Ghost's entrance after the killing. Polonius's body lies as silent witness to Hamlet's capacity for swift action, yet Hamlet accuses himself as 'your tardy son' and the Ghost replies: 'Do not forget. This visitation/ Is but to whet thy almost blunted purpose' (III.iv.110–11). Here the effect of the apparition must surely contrast with that of its earlier hauntings. There, its revelation in a martial context merged with and enhanced Hamlet's sense of an unnatural world; here, Gertrude's presence shows it as intruding in that world, while Polonius's body and its apparent irrelevance to both Ghost and Hamlet show a drastic double standard developing in Hamlet, as obsession with the past blinds his judgement of the present. True, towards the close of the scene he can say: 'For this same lord/ I do repent; but heaven hath pleas'd it so,/ To punish me with this and this with me,/ That I must be their scourge and minister' (III.iv.174–7). But Polonius here appears only as part of the greater design in which Hamlet is absorbed, and this speech comes perilously close to the hubris of the later Othello. In the end Polonius is dismissed lightly: 'This man shall set me packing./ I'll lug the guts into the neighbour room./

. . . This counsellor/ Is now most still, most secret, and most grave,/ Who was in life a foolish prating knave' (III.iv.213–17). The corpse is no *memento mori* for Hamlet, when a ghost and father gilded with heroic images compound Hamlet's divorce from nature.

Yet there is irony in the fact that, while Polonius might act as *memento mori* for Claudius, the king is too worldly to see this as he showed at prayer. He certainly perceives the threat to his survival ('It had been so with us had we been there', IV.i.13), but he is as blind to the emblematic status of this corpse as Rosencrantz and Guildenstern will be (IV.ii.4–29) and as Hamlet is. The reason for this failure of traditional *memento mori* becomes clear when Hamlet faces Claudius: for the audience, Hamlet certainly fulfills the function of professional fool in his discourse on Death the leveller (IV.iii.19–31); but the peculiar stress on the fate of 'a king' presents this as a threat to a Claudius by now obsessed with guilt and the determination to survive. Ironically, too, this discourse parallels much of Hamlet's meditation over Yorick, but there is a crucial difference of emphasis, and therefore of effect on audience and characters alike: with Claudius, Hamlet's argument moves from the general to the particular, with clear implications for Claudius; with Yorick, the argument moves from the skull as type to the skull as acknowledged fool where type and individual inform each other. The effect on Hamlet himself will be very different as a result.

Now the play moves from the court to Hamlet's glimpse of Fortinbras. Much has been made of the structural parallels between Hamlet and Fortinbras, Hamlet and Laertes: his two contemporaries have frequently been seen as men of action countering Hamlet's tardiness, as on one level they appear to do. Yet the parallels are not developed simply: Fortinbras does not avenge his father, but bows to his uncle's will and sets out on a pursuit of honour not unlike Hotspur's; Laertes abandons spontaneity and resorts to treachery under Claudius's guidance. But, quite apart from Hamlet's insistence on his own tardiness, there seems to me a most important difference: for both Fortinbras and Laertes, the play provides historically attested reasons for revenge, by report in Fortinbras's case, by the evidence of the action in Laertes's. Both are restrained by liege lords whose right to command they both acknowledge. Both then remain men of the world, where unnatural acts threaten but do not totally destroy their natural world. Hamlet's case is quite other. The natural world has become unnatural for him when he first speaks, and he has no-one capable of restoring him to the world until the carefully prepared advent of Yorick. His reason for vengeance is never naturally revealed to him: his father's murder is announced by a ghost; his liege lord and mother are implicated. The 'play' may produce guilty reaction, but since the murderer in that 'play' is specified as nephew to the king, Claudius's response could stem as much from Hamlet's future threat as from his own guilty past. The audience is given the facts in the prayer scene, but the action is careful to stress that Hamlet's interpretation of what he sees is far astray. So Hamlet's 'revenge' lies on a level of speculation far removed from that of Fortinbras and Laertes as, unlike them, he has all natural yardsticks specifically removed by the development of the action, until the Gravedigger's scene.

This scene changes the whole tone of the play. Too often, the planning of the deaths of Rosencrantz and Guildenstern, the return from England, and the change in Hamlet's attitudes are treated chronologically rather than in theatre sequence, which is the only valid sequence for critics. In the action, the Gravedigger and his companion appear on stage before Hamlet himself. The play shows good reason for this: the Gravedigger establishes himself as master of a zany logic parodying Hamlet's earlier antic disposition. Moreover his subject is death, with the world's ways cheerfully mocked. In some sixty-five lines, he presents a world free from ghosts, where a stoup of liquor, a lovesong, and a grave (as in *Twelfth Night*) are natural cohabitants, and 'The houses he makes lasts till doomsday' (V.i.59). When Hamlet arrives, two skulls are to hand, and Hamlet meditates on Death the leveller by way of types familiar from the Dance of Death: one 'might be the pate of a politician' or of a courtier (V.i.76–85), the other the skull of a lawyer (V.i.96), all three stock creatures of the Machiavellian society the Gravedigger has already derided and dismissed by his proclaimed kinship with Adam (V.i.29–31). The effect of Hamlet's meditations is very different from his comments on death in IV.iii, both visually and in tone. Here the basic commonness of skulls, their appearance on stage, gives Hamlet *memento mori* emblems he can interpret without ambivalence for the first time in the play.

When he turns to the Gravedigger, he faces a mirror image of his old skills in quibbling, and has to admit defeat: 'We must speak by the card or equivocation will undo us' (V.i.133). He is almost ready for his next crucial encounter, as the Gravedigger has pointed the Fool's way eloquently. For the Gravedigger, after confronting Hamlet casually with his own 'madness', goes on to discuss his trade and, by way of illustration, produces the skull of 'a whoreson mad fellow', 'a mad rogue', 'Yorick's skull, the King's jester' (V.i.170–5).

Yorick's is the last and only named skull. In Yorick, Hamlet meets, as it were, the *memento mori* of the 'transi' tomb and of portraiture. A transi tomb in its most familiar form is a double monument: above lies an effigy in full earthly regalia, below lies a cadaver or skeleton (the transi)[5]. So the dead man is shown at the two extremes of his mortal lot: above, with the rank and dignity that have won him respect and below, levelled by death. One of several native examples is Henry Chichele's tomb in Canterbury Cathedral (the Archbishop of Shakespeare's *Henry V*). In portraiture too, the skull figures frequently, and this fashion in art was particularly popular at the time of *Hamlet*'s creation.[6] And alongside the images of death linked with the identifiable living, The Dance of Death was continuously popular throughout mediaeval and renaissance times. In this tradition too is *The Daunce and Song of Death*, a broadside of 1569, where a king leads the line of dancers and a fool brings up the rear[7].

In all these cases, the visual links with the structure of *Hamlet* are strong. While the first two skulls are types, in Yorick type and individual merge and unite. For the first time in the play, Hamlet recalls memories of boyhood: 'He hath bore me on his back a thousand times . . . Here hung those lips that I have kissed I know not how oft' (V.i.179–83). He teases Yorick with his skull's estate and urges the Fool to act as *memento mori* for others: 'Now get you to my lady's chamber and tell her, let her paint an inch thick, to this favour she must come' (V.i.186–8). This is indeed one part of the message of the transi tomb and the death's head in portraiture. The recognizable personal form which predominates in both forms of visual art should not make us underestimate the common significance of the skull. And, importantly for the play, Hamlet's disgust at Yorick's skull is a natural disgust of the senses, quite unlike the rising hysteria of his meeting with the Ghost.

---

[5] See Kathleen Cohen, *Metamorphosis of a Death Symbol: The Transi Tomb in the Late Middle Ages and the Renaissance* (University of California Press, Berkeley Los Angeles, London, 1973). My thanks to Pamela King of the Dept of English, Westfield College, for pointing out this connection.

[6] See, for example, Roy Strong, *The English Icon: Elizabethan and Jacobean Portraiture* (The Paul Mellon Foundation for British Art, 1969. London, Routledge and Kegan Paul Ltd; New York, Pantheon Books).

[7] For a useful account of this, see the New Mermaid Edition of *The Revenger's Tragedy*, ed. Brian Gibbons (1967).

Turning from the skull, Hamlet pursues its message, considering the inevitable absurdity awaiting heroes in death. When Horatio objects to his line of thought (' 'Twere to consider too curiously to consider so', V.i.199, echoing Hamlet's earlier concern over the abuse of reason as 'some craven scruple/ Of thinking too precisely on th' event', IV.iv.40–1), Hamlet replies: 'No, faith, not a jot, but to follow him thither with modesty enough, and likelihood to lead it' (V.i.200–1). It is in terms of the idea of the play that Hamlet considers heroes after encountering Yorick. All his images for his father have been superhuman; Horatio the sceptic's account of the old king upheld this view, and the 'majestical' armed Ghost reaffirmed it. Now Hamlet's absurdist speculations on Alexander and Caesar mark the natural end of these inflated images: old Hamlet and the Ghost are laid and cease to interfere in the action of the play. Yorick's work as the old King's Fool is well done, and could only be done by a dead Fool.

For the Ghost and Yorick act as structural poles in the play. The Ghost goaded Hamlet with 'thoughts beyond the reaches of our souls', thoughts which threatened to make Hamlet's dispossession and dislocation permanent; the *memento mori* of Yorick the Fool brings him, almost literally, down to earth again. After confronting Yorick, Hamlet re-enters the world of men, for better or worse. At Ophelia's grave he names himself for the first time (V.i.250–1); and ironically his irrational outburst here asserts the reasonableness of Polonius's explanation for his madness: 'I lov'd Ophelia' (V.i.264). Too late for father and daughter, he reacts with a kind of madness that social convention may deplore but accept as natural: the madness of the lover. Moreover, Hamlet seems here to dissociate himself from the consequences of his former actions when he says to Laertes: 'Hear you, sir,/ What is the reason that you use me thus?/ I lov'd you ever' (V.i.283–5), a dissociation he makes more explicit in the final scene (V.ii.222–40). It would seem that he expects Laertes to treat his grievances as purged by Hamlet's own repudiation of his madness. Yet, as in *The Winter's Tale* where Antigonus's fatal mission is not stopped by Leontes's recovery of his senses, Hamlet's past actions cannot be undone. This is underlined by the revelation of the fate of Rosencrantz and Guildenstern, importantly only after the Grave-digger's scene. Unlike Polonius, ironically enough, they are not forgotten by Hamlet, who now sees their deaths as part of a straight-forward conflict between Claudius and himself (V.ii.57–62). They remain part of the natural world he has re-entered which, as for

Laertes, houses but is not entirely swamped by unnatural acts. The killing of Polonius, instrumental to Hamlet's death, seems purged from his mind with the supernatural and superhuman King. For after Yorick, the Ghost evaporates; in these last moments of the play traditional Providence replaces it. When Hamlet refers to his father's murder, it is in terms of public responsibility, not revenge; for he examines judicially the growth of evil in relation to present and future, not lingering obsessively over the past:

> Does it not, think thee, stand me now upon—
> He that hath kill'd my king and whor'd my mother,
> Popp'd in between th'election and my hopes,
> Thrown out his angle for my proper life
> And with such coz'nage—is't not perfect conscience
> To quit him with this arm? And is't not to be damn'd
> To let this canker of our nature come
> In further evil?                                    (V.ii.63–70)

Indeed, the final duel and its consequences underline this. Claudius's immediate treachery embraces foil and cup, and by foil and cup he is killed. The vengeance Hamlet is seen and heard to take is for unnatural acts in the course of the duel scene. The play itself may avenge the Ghost; Hamlet avenges and pays for worldly acts. After meeting Yorick, he is released from the supernatural and superhuman to take action in human terms. The arrival of Fortinbras acts as corollary: the heroics and hauntings are over, so that Horatio can utter his final prayer within a convention that does not seem ridiculous and Fortinbras comes not as threat but promise. Yorick indeed has his place in *Hamlet*.

# II

# William Patten: A Tudor Londoner

## BETTY HILL

Three years after the *Mary Rose* foundered and the Lord Admiral, the Earl of Warwick, burnt up Treport and diverse villages with the loss of only David Googan, the most detailed contemporary account of the Pinkie Campaign of August to September 1547 appeared in diary form. This work was put out by Richard Grafton[1] of Greyfriars, printer to Edward VI, as *The expedicion into Scotla(n)de of the most woorthely fortunate prince Edward, Duke of Soomerset . . . made in the first yere of his Maiesties most prosperous reign and set out by way of diarie, by W. Patten Londoner.*[2] The author gives his full name as William Patten in his dedication as a 'moste bounden client and puple' to his patron Sir William Paget, who, three years before his death in 1563, was known to Bishop Bale and Archbishop Parker as a private collector of manuscripts.[3] The expedition made by Protector Somerset, in continuation of his policy of 'rough wooing' of the Scots, included William Wynter and, as the two 'Judges of the Marshalsey', administrators of martial law, Patten and William Cecil.

In his preface Patten gives as his reason for publication his general judgement that everybody wants to know about their valiant victory over their enemies, because from both his learning and nature he understands 'þe thursty desyer, that all our kynde hath to knowe'. The Pinkie Campaign had been a general subject of conversation since his return, and he had been asked so many questions about it 'as would haue wel cumbered a righte ripetunged deponent redyly to aunswer'. In his conclusion he excuses his delay in producing the publication expected of him, though he would have liked to delay it

---

[1] For the printers and booksellers mentioned throughout see E. Gordon Duff, *A century of the English book trade 1457–1557* (London, 1905); *A dictionary of printers and booksellers in England . . . 1557–1640*, Bibliographical Society. (London, 1910).

[2] References are to the Bodleian Library copy. For a modernized text see E. Arber, *The English Garner* III (London, 1880), pp. 51–155.

[3] C.E. Wright, 'The Dispersal of the Monastic Libraries and the beginnings of Anglo-Saxon Studies', *Transactions of the Cambridge Bibliographical Society* 1 (1951), 214.

longer. For he had failed to make sufficient notes on the spot about the precise observation of words, deeds, and gestures, and to diligently mark the topographical details, and so he had had to search his memory. Cecil and he had only discovered before they left for home that they had been making independent notes, and Cecil had communicated his own notes to him since their return. He has given us three hours' reading 'to make you censour of my three moneths wryting: Judge ye I pray you (as ye maye) with fauour, and conster my meanyng to the best'.

I have written elsewhere of Patten, a great-nephew of Waynflete, founder of Magdalen College, Oxford, because of his later association with a manuscript of late twelfth-century English texts, generally designated *The Trinity Homilies*.[4] But the *Expedicion* is his first acknowledged work, and his mention, in conclusion, of his residence at the Parsonage of St Mary-at-Hill on 28 January 1548, provides a useful biographical pointer. Since, as my study of the records of St Mary-at-Hill, Billingsgate revealed, Patten became a *conduct* 'organist' or 'male chorister' there in 1528, he must have been born about 1510 to 1512. The *Expedicion* is also important because it illustrates and partly explains two inseparable facets of the man—the tenor of his long life and the kind and variety of his work, both published and unpublished. Patten was already sensible of what was expected of him and of what he was capable of.

His interest in linguistic differences appears, for example, from his quotations (C vii recto, G viii verso) of Warwick's retort when the Scots attempted to ambush him: 'Why . . . wil not these *knaves* be ruled?' and the Scottish taunts of 'cum here *loundes*, cum here *tykes*, . . .' [italics mine]. His use of similes reveals his sense of decorum. Anything he could say in praise of Somerset's excellent deeds 'should rather obscure and darken them, and as it wear washe iuery with inke' (pref.), and on the English side there was 'a generall rumor ꝝ buzzing amoong þe souldiours, not vnlyke þe nois of þe sea beyng harde a far of' (F vii recto). The behaviour of the Scots, however, is described in terms of animal imagery. The Scottish pikes bristled so thickly 'that as easly shall a bare fynger perce thrugh the skyn of an angrie hedgehog, as ony encounter the frunt of their pykes' (G iv verso); and across Fauxside Bray they came across a 'Castel or pile' with Scots inside who, when they saw their side driven away, 'pluct

⁴ 'Trinity College Cambridge MS. B. 14. 52, and William Patten', *TCBS* 4 (1966), 192–200. I repeat here some of the material, pp. 196–9, with some addition and without further reference to the sources given there.

in their peces, lyke a dog his taile: and couched themselfes within all muet' (L ii recto). Patten attempts restraint in describing the behaviour of the Borderers, whom he suspects of being in collusion with the Scots, in keeping him awake at night in camp, with their commotion trying to find their Captains, 'not vnlyke (to be playn) vnto a masterles hound howlyng in a hie wey when he hath lost him he wayted on' (L iv verso).

Patten, also, is capable both of a lively detailed description of places and persons, suggestive of a down-to-earth Englisher, given to keen observation but not undue sentiment, and of an erudite discussion of graver matters fitting to the Age. He describes the descent from Fauxside Bray into a 'lane or strete of a xxx. foot brode, fenced on eyther syde with a wall of turf an elle of height', which led north near St Michael's Undreske on a hill somewhat higher than the camp (E iv recto); and he records Somerset chancing on:

> a fellowe lyke a man, but I wot not of what sorte, smal of stature, redhedded, curld rounde about ⁊ shedded afore, of a xl. yere old, ⁊ calde himself Knockes. To say sumwhat of his hauour, his cote was of þe coulor of a wel burnt brik (I mean not blak) ⁊ wel worth xx.d. a brode yarde, it was pretely fresed, half with an ado ⁊ hemmed round about very sutably with pasmai lace of grene caddis, me thought he represented þe state of a sumner in sum citee or of a pedler in sum boorowe. (C viii verso–D j recto).

On Friday, 9 September, Gorgon's day, Patten toys long (D vi verso–viii recto) with the identification of Gorgon 'eyther so obscure that no man knowes him, or els so aunciente as euery man forgettes him'. He *would* like to discuss him but doesn't know what to make of him, 'a he saint a she sainte or a neuter (for we haue all in oure Kallendar)'. In his digression (A vi recto–B j verso) on Protector Somerset's dream of a few nights back, he mentions the three theories about dreams held by the astronomers, Plato and the physicians, and the theologians. He concludes that Somerset had an Allegoric dream in which the events dreamt of turn out to be the exact opposite in reality. But as a Biblical example of a Speculative dream, in which events are accurately foreshadowed, he mentions from *Genesis*, ch. xli, how seven plentiful years and seven years of famine in Egypt were signified to Pharaoh as seven fat oxen and seven full ears of corn and seven lean oxen and seven withered ears.

Already in 1547–8 Patten shows a predilection for Old Testament sevens, a trend which reappeared nearly thirty years later in his *The calender of scripture*, in which Biblical names of whatever derivation were 'put into our English for oour Cuntrey, which was the cheef cause of the trauayl taken'. His entry under *Elizabeth* reads '*Heb. Arquer*. Dei mei Saturitas. Dei mei Iusiurandum. Dei mei Septimum: The fulness of my God. The oth of my God. The Seauenth of my God.' This is followed by a long digression in Latin on the number *seven*, which is made from 1 and 6, 2 and 5, and 3 and 4, the last pair being the vehicle of human life since the body is composed of four elements and the mind of three components. Patten then details human development in months by sevens and years by sevens. The seven Ages are linked with the seven planets, and we are introduced to other sets of sevens, including the Arts, provinces, kingdoms, Pleiads, Ages of the world, and Pauline Epistles. This obsession with sevens, reinforced by the climate of the Age and the requirements of the cult of Elizabeth, later appeared in his two broadsides of the 1580s and 1590s, both addressed to the Queen.

In the *Expedicion* Patten also indicates the importance he attaches to the remembrance of friends. His description (K vi verso–vii verso) of the Scottish atrocities includes mention of Edward Shelley, Lieutenant of the men-at-arms of Boulogne, who was recognizable only by his beard: 'so nere my frende . . . I thinke his merit to mooch to be let pas in silence . . . I trust it shall not be taken that I mean hearby to derogate fame from ony of the rest that dyed thear.'

My previous study established Patten's authorship of three printed works:

1. *The expedicion*. *STC* 19476.5.[5]
2. *The calender of scripture*. *H & L* C4.[6] This was printed as an anonymous work in 1575 by Richard Jugge, who was jointly with Cawood, printer to Queen Elizabeth and conducted his business in Newgate Market. But it is mentioned as a 'Calender of the Bible' in a letter in a sixteenth-century cursive script on fol. 1 verso of *The Trinity Homilies* as the work of one knowledgeable in Armenian and author of the six Latin verses above. This Latin poem, written above the letter, is identifiable as Patten's work by the signature 'W P',[7]

---

[5] *STC* references are to *A short-title catalogue of books . . . 1475–1640* 2nd ed., rev. by W. A. Jackson, *et al*. II, I–Z (London, 1976). Volume I is forthcoming.

[6] *H & L* references are to S. Halkett & J. Laing, *A dictionary of anonymous and pseudonymous publications . . .* 3rd ed. rev. by John Horden. I, 1475–1640 (Harlow, 1980).

[7] The poem, initials and letter are reproduced in facsimile in *TCBS* 4, plate XVII, facing p. 195.

which is identical to that of 'W P(atten)' in his manuscript *Names expoounded* . . . (see 6 below). The *Calender* includes, under the discussion of the name *Elizabeth,* a revised version of the first three hundred lines or so of Patten's manuscript *Supplicatio* (see 5 below).

3. *In mortem W. Wynter equitis aurati.*[8] *STC* 19477. This pamphlet of four leaves is signed on the last leaf 'Olim socius . . . Amicus semper . . . W. Patten, Gen.' These Latin verses were printed in 1589 by Thomas Orwin, who traded in Pater Noster Row near the Exchequer and had been apprenticed to Thomas Purfoote senior.

Patten's three manuscript works are:

4. April 1570. An alphabet and vocabulary [for reading Archbishop Parker's Armenian Psalter], Corpus Christi College, Cambridge Small Parker 281A.[9] A note on fol. iii verso, badly cropped, reads '[H]unc alphabetum elaboratum & scriptum cum [L]exico Armenico manu & diligentia Mr̄i [P]aten Londinensis . . .'

5. 16 November 1572. *Supplicatio Patteni.* Latin verse. BL MS. Lansdowne 739. A note at the end reads 'Exscripsit decennis filiolus Tho. Patten.'

6. January 1584. *Names expoounded of certein regionz 7 places.* English prose. Cambridge University Library MS. Dd. XI. 40. An autograph etymological glossary of place-names. The dedication of January 1584 to Sir Thomas Bromley, who was Lord Chancellor from 1579 to 1587, is signed on fol. 5 verso 'W. Patten'.

The pursuit of several thousand sixteenth-century items for the revised edition of Halkett and Laing happily resulted in an important article by Brian O'Kill.[10] From his study of Patten's printed works and the published volumes of the *Calendar of Patent Rolls,* Dr O'Kill threw further light on our author's literary and public activities. These, he felt, heightened the interest of Patten's work to historians, linguists, and bibliographers, in compensation for his loss of a moral stance sustained for nearly four centuries and his emergence in the late twentieth as a feckless chap, 'not only a scholar, historian, and

[8] Professor Bruce Dickins anonymously added this find to *TCBS* 4, p. 200.

[9] Formerly item 4 in Small Parker 281, described by M.R. James, *A descriptive catalogue of the manuscripts in the library of Corpus Christi College, Cambridge* II (Cambridge, 1912), pp. 420–1. Item 4 was separated in 1973 and put in an envelope made by Mr Barnes to match the binding of Small Parker 281.

[10] 'The printed works of William Patten (*c* 1510–*c* 1600)', *TCBS* 7 (1977), 28–45.

bilingual poetaster, but a satirist, spelling-reformer, and peculator, surviving the bizarre twists of fortune for about ninety years' (p. 28). Dr O'Kill's intensive work on library holdings clinched the assembled contemporary evidence I have given above of Patten's authorship of *The calender of scripture*, for the inscription on the title-page of the Harvard University Library copy reads 'W. Patten Author et Possessor' (p. 30). He also provided résumés of the content of Patten's printed works and quotations from them, illustrative of his well-known orthographical peculiarities and his use of archaic and abstruse vocabulary.

Moreover, Dr O'Kill added six works to the Patten canon, two English prose and four verse pieces, two of which are still ascribed to William Painter in the revised *STC*. He tentatively assigns to Patten *The late expedicion in Scotlande . . .* of 1544, *H & L* L25, which shows some of the stylistic and lexical features of Patten's known works. But, more intriguingly, since the mystification of the *raison d'être* and of some bibliographical matters still remains, he presents Patten as the author of *Laneham's Letter, H & L* L55. This work purports to be a *Letter* addressed by Robert Laneham or Langham, Clerk of the Council Chamber (whose existence can be verified from the Public Records) to 'Master Humphrey Martin mercer', describing part of the Queen's entertainment in July 1575 at Kenilworth Castle, provided by Robert Dudley, Earl of Leicester. It is a lively, amusing account, which complements and contrasts with George Gascoigne's description of part of the festivities, the most spectacular in the whole of Elizabeth's reign, in *The princelye pleasures at Kenelworth Castle*.[11]

Dr O'Kill, in supporting Patten's authorship, points out (p. 36) that on pages 13–14 of the Huntington Library copy of the *Letter*[12] are nine lines of Latin verse welcoming the Queen, which were fixed over the Castle gate in a frame and which Gascoigne attributes to 'master Paten'. I take this point further. For Gascoigne (Nichols, pp. 492–3) prints in this context thirteen lines of verse beginning 'Jupiter è summi dum vertice cernit Olympi' and ending 'Castrumque Kenelmi', composed by Master Muncaster, and states that 'Master

---

[11] Both printed in J. Nichols, *The progresses . . . of Queen Elizabeth* 2nd. ed. (London, 1823), I, pp. 420–84, 485–523. For other editions of the *Letter* see Scott (n. 13 below), 297, n.2, and add R.J.P. Kuin (Amsterdam, 1973).

[12] Reproduced in facsimile, *English Linguistics 1500–1800*, ed. R.C. Alston. No. 60 (Menston, 1968).

Paten' also devised verses to the same effect. Gascoigne is not sure whether Muncaster's or 'Paten's' were pronounced, but they were all to one effect. This is so, for Patten's nine lines quoted in the *Letter* begin 'Iupiter huc certes cernens TE tendere gressus' and end '& werda Kenelmi'. Patten naturally included in the *Letter* his own composition, not Muncaster's. This and three lines headed *De Regina Nostra Illvstrissima* on the title page and the four lines entitled *De Maiestate Regia*, which conclude the work on p. 87, can be added to Patten's Latin output in praise of Elizabeth. Dr O'Kill adduces such other evidences of authorship as (1) verbal echoes of *The calender of scripture* (1575), including a familiar reference to the interpretation of *Elizabeth* as 'the Seaventh of my God'; (2) Patten's distinctive orthography, lexis, special interests, and stylistic effects which are evident in the *Letter* as elsewhere; and (3) some manuscript emendations and additions in the Huntington Library copy in Patten's hand. He admirably clinches his case by quoting (p. 38) Patten's somewhat conspiratorial letter to Cecil of 10 September 1575. This concerns the suppression of 'the book' because Langham had complained and because Patten does not want to make a jest of the entertainment provided to honour the Queen.

David Scott, in a partly overlapping study published in the same year,[13] based part of his case for Patten's authorship of the *Letter* on the resemblances between that work and the *Expedicion* in respect of the persona of the author, formal and comic description of people and edifices, the incidence of alliteration and use of extended metaphors; and he elucidates the genesis of the authority of the name 'Laneham'. Both Dr O'Kill, tentatively, and Professor Scott, enthusiastically, bear in mind the possibility of a young Will Shakespeare at Kenilworth in July 1575, and of a remembrance of such splendours as a mermaid on a dolphin in *A Midsummer Night's Dream* (II. i. 148–68).

Professor Scott usefully reproduces (facing page 302) specimens of Patten's secretary and cursive hands dating from about 1580. There are specimens of both kinds of later dates in the Public Record Office,[14] and of Patten's cursive script of an earlier date in *The Trinity Homilies*, where he added interlinear English glosses to the early

[13] 'William Patten and the authorship of "Robert Laneham's *Letter*" (1575)', *ELR* 7 (1977), 297–306.
[14] 1583, secretary hand, STAC 5 W29/32, Patten's answer to a bill of complaint by Thomas Waskat; 1595, cursive hand, STAC 5 P33/15, Questions to be asked of James Jakes in respect of Dorothy Constable.

Middle English texts. In this connection it is worth remembering Dr
O'Kill's mention (p. 37) of Patten's use of archaisms of Old English
origin. The relationship between this usage and his reading and
glossing of twelfth-century English needs some investigation. So do
other aspects of Patten's language, and his practices in relation
to sixteenth-century attitudes towards the enrichment of the vernacular, and the fitness of the vocabulary and style of those subjects
proper to English prose. Such matters apart, I support these critics'
views on the authorship of the *Letter*, not only on the kinds of
evidence they bring forward, but because the *Expedicion* and the
*Letter* seem to me to evince the same ebullient sense of fun which
appeared to surface when the two Williams, Patten the Londoner,
and Cecil, the Stamford squire's son, were together in *uplondish*
places. But I reserve the delights of the Lady of the Lake, the seal of
Islington, Captain Cox with his borrowed velvet cap and two-
handed sword, and the Italian fireworks, which 'woold have made
mee, for my part, az hardy az I am, very veangeably afeard' (Nichols,
p. 435) for another occasion.

To Patten's elegy on Wynter, Dr O'Kill (pp. 32–4) adds two
others. *A moorning diti* in English verse, *H & L* M161, was composed
in 1580 on the death of Henry Fitzalan, the 12th Earl of Arundel, a
collector and lender of manuscripts,[15] with whom Patten had served
as secretary at Boulogne. Patten's Latin verses *Luctus consolatorius*
(see *H & L* A113), printed by Orwin in 1591, lament the death of
Christopher Hatton. He had succeeded Thomas Bromley as Lord
Chancellor, and was a friend and patron of men of letters, and a
devoté of Elizabeth. Patten apparently regards Arundel, the soldier,
Wynter, the sailor, and Hatton, the courtier, as among those 'whoo
. . . (in my opinion) towarde his prince and cuntree did best deserue'
(*Expedicion*, K vii verso).

The remaining two items in the Patten canon, *H & L* F47, A113,
are both translations of Latin psalms into seven English septenaries,
addressed to Elizabeth. The first, composed in 1583, the twenty-fifth
year of her reign, when Accession Day fell on a Sunday and Whitgift
preached to the Great,[16] was printed by Abel Jeffes at the sign of the
Bell in Fore Street near Grub Street. The second, a translation of the
twenty-first 'terseptimus' psalm, Patten's last known work, made in

---

[15] Wright, 'Dispersal', 214; R. Flower, 'Laurence Nowell and the discovery of England in Tudor times', *PBA* (1935), p. 54.
[16] Roy Strong, *The Cult of Elizabeth* (Wallop, Hampshire, 1977), p. 124.

1598, was printed by Thomas Purfoote junior, possibly at the sign of
the Lucrece, within the new rents in Newgate Market. The original
roll for presentation, BL MS. Royal 14 B L, signed in Patten's
secretary hand 'Humilimus et Devotus/ WP. G.', was clearly an
Accession Day tribute in celebration of the XLIst year of the glorious
reign of 'She (by name) the Seaventh of my God' . . .

> thearby too yeeld God all
> dutifull thanks four our Queenz singuler
> prudent Goovernauns eeven too this
> present Annuall Seaventeenth of
> November, the happy day of
> entrauns intoo her gracioous
> Rein.

Considering the excesses of Accession Day, of which Sir Roy
Strong (pp. 114–28) has given such an excellent account, and the
multitude of names under which Elizabeth was praised, Patten's
adulations are spare and subdued. What could be more scholarly *and*
respectful than the third Hebraic signification 'the Seaventh of my
God'?

Patten's only other known work addressed to Elizabeth is the
*Supplicatio*, presented to and accepted by the Queen at the Hampton
Court festivities on Sunday, 16 November 1572, the Eve of Accession Day. Patten asks for compassion on his destitution, and refers
(pp. 11 verso, 12 verso) to his recent twenty months of unhappiness
following his almost twenty years of public offices and social status
at Stoke Newington, between 1550 and 1570. Both Dr O'Kill and I
have written independently about Patten at Stoke Newington and
his eventual loss, as a debtor to the Crown, of his offices and home.
Patten again stresses his sense of identity as a Londoner, 'Vrbs mihi
sit natale solu*m* celeberrima London' (p. 15 recto); and his fellow–
Londoner John Stow, who subsequently included Patten in his
'Honour of citizens, and worthiness of men in the same', mentioned
his restoration (in 1563) of Stoke Newington church.

Although Patten, as J. P. for Middlesex, was responsible for
maintaining the Queen's Peace, three indictments exist against him
and others in the Session rolls for 25 May 1566, 25 May 1568 and 2
April 1569 for breaking into Robert Harrington's land.[17] There is

---

[17] Greater London Record Office MJ/SR 156/14, 156/13, 156/15. The
indictment against Harrington is 152/25. J. C. Jeaffreson, *Middlesex County*

also an indictment in the Session roll 21 March 1568 against Robert Harrington, clerk, two labourers and a carpenter, all of Harnesey, Middlesex, for breaking into Patten's close at Stoke Newington and treading down his grass. In return (Session roll 2 April 1569), Patten, with a yeoman, and an anonymous rabble, and arms and violence, broke into Harrington's freehold close called 'Lyttle Kyngsfyeld', parcel of the prebend of Browneswood of St Paul's, London, put Harrington off his land and kept him out. This indictment has a preamble or recital, referring to the Act of Parliament 8 Henry VI. c.9 concerning forcible entry, and a statement at the bottom that John Southecott, Justice of the Common Pleas, and Thomas Wroth, Kt., gave judgement on 7 July 1569 that the land should be restored to its rightful owner. There is no mention of a penalty being imposed on Patten.

For William Patten two interests remained—manuscripts and joint-stock companies. It is not clear as to how much contact he had with Cecil's household in the Strand, which in the 1560s included Laurence Nowell, the brother of Alexander, the Dean of St Paul's and of Richard, Attorney-General of the Court of Wards of which Cecil was Master. Laurence Nowell, a member of Archbishop Parker's household, became Tutor to Cecil's ward, Edward de Vere, the 17th Earl of Oxford, in 1563. Cecil himself was a collector and restorer of manuscripts on the same lines as, and comparable with, Parker and his workmen at Lambeth Palace. The two men were close friends and they are known to have exchanged manuscripts between 1566 and 1573.[18] Patten was certainly acquainted with Parker who preached at Stoke Newington in 1560. As he writes in his *Supplicatio*, p. 22 recto, 'Archipraesul sacra cui Dorouernia sedes Integrum Dauidis Psalterium mihi monstrat.' This must have been between 1566 and early 1570 when Patten compiled his alphabet and vocabulary (Small Parker 281A) from that same Armenian Psalter. He was also known to the Archbishop as a borrower or collector of manuscripts, for Parker, who died in 1575, referred in a marginal note on p. 264 of Corpus Christi College, Cambridge MS. 51 to a *Supple-*

Records I (1886), pp. 62, 64, in printing only 152/25 (21 March 1568) and 156/15 (2 April 1569), misrepresents the case. I am indebted to Miss Joan Coburn, Deputy Head Archivist, for notice of 156/13–14 and for the further information about 156/15 (letter of 28 June 1976).

[18] Wright, 'Dispersal', 218–19, 220, n.1, 221, 233, 236; W.W. Greg, 'Books and bookmen in the correspondence of Archbishop Parker', *The Library* 4th series, 16 (1936), 273–4.

*mentum Sigiberti* as being in the possession of Patten in the parish of Aldermanbury.

It appears, then, that Patten had moved there from Stoke Newington. He certainly never returned to his old home which he had assigned to John Dudley in 1571. Dudley's widow lived at the Manor of Stoke Newington until her death in 1602 with her second husband Thomas Sutton, who, nine years later, founded Charterhouse School.[19] In 1568 Patten had become associated with two joint-stock companies financed from London. One of these was the Mines Royal, with which, among others, Cecil, Wynter, and John Dudley were connected, which had the sole right of mining for precious metal and copper in Cumberland, Wales, and Cornwall. The other was the Mineral and Battery Works, which had the sole right to mine calamine and make brass.[20] It was from Aldermanbury that Patten wrote in 1580 about the institution of the parts of the Mines Royal to Sir Francis Walsingham,[21] the Queen's 'Sir Moor', who was the head of the Elizabethan 'Circus' with a network of thirty-five agents.[22]

Although Patten's movements between 1580 and 1599 are not entirely clear, there is evidence that between 1590 and 1598–9 he was a member of the Elizabethan Society of Antiquaries. On 27 November 1590 he contributed a few notes on the antiquity and exposition of the word *sterling* for discussion with John Stow, Francis Tate and Richard Broughton, both of the Inner Temple, Michael Heneage and Thomas Talbot, both connected with the Records in the Tower, Arthur Agarde of the Exchequer, and with the others who wrote papers on the same subject. Patten also attended two meetings of the Society on 21 February and 13 May 1591, and was summoned to another in 1598–9.

By 1599 Patten may have been living with Ann, his seventh child,[23] in the parish of St Bartholomew the Great close by Smithfield. On 6 July of that year he was granted letters of administration

---

[19] W. Robinson, *The history and antiquities of the parish of Stoke Newington* (London, 1820), p. 29, n.f; G.S. Davies, *Charterhouse in London* (London, 1921), p. 160.

[20] *Calendar of Patent Rolls*, 1566–9, nos. 1195, 1589. See further A.L. Rowse, *The England of Elizabeth* (London, 1950; repr. 1961), pp. 124–6, 152.

[21] P.R.O. SP 12/144, 68–70.

[22] Paul Johnson, *Elizabeth I* (London, 1974), pp. 276–7.

[23] According to J. Foster, *Pedigrees of the county families of England* I. Lancashire (London, 1873), Patten of Bank Hall.

of her estate,[24] but three, at least, of his sons outlived him. Gratien died in 1603 in the parish of St Andrew, Holborn.[25] His eldest son Mercury, who became Bluemantle Pursuivant of Arms in 1597, under Cecil's patronage, was a calligrapher of note.[26] He was responsible for two gift books containing illuminations of the arms, and accompanied by verses descriptive of the different arms and quarterings, crests and supporters, of their recipients. Mercury's work for Lord North is now Bodleian MS. North e 24; the book for Thomas [Howard], Earl of Suffolk, is extant as Cambridge University Library MS. Add. 7092. Mercury, who was an indifferent attender at the College, sold his office in 1611 and died in 1622.[27]

Thomas, who at the age of ten had acted as his father's amanuensis for the *Supplicatio*, and had also written out the Latin poem on fol. 1 verso of *The Trinity Homilies*, apparently shared his father's interest in manuscripts and his propensity for destitution. In 1587 he purchased BL MS. Royal 17 C XX (see fol. 2 recto) from [Gregory] Seton, the bookseller under Aldersgate. BL MS. Add. 5750 (new fol. 43, 42) relates to his office for the years 1603–4 as Clerk of the Closet to Queen Anne of Denmark; but after her death in 1619 he lost the office he had held for twenty-six years and was left destitute.[28] Thomas died in the parish of St Margaret, Westminster in 1637, and on 4 February of that year letters of administration of his estate were granted to Thomas Beshey, Mary Patten his widow remaining.[29] Thomas Patten's manuscript (see fol. 4 verso) was bought by John Theyer in May 1640 from Bailey, the Holborn bookseller. That Theyer was the great-grandson of Thomas Theyer and his wife Agnes, née Hart, the sister of John Hart, the last Prior of Lanthony.

[24] P.R.O. Prob. 6/6, 19 verso. I owe the modern references to the Probate documents, which were in Somerset House in the early 1960s, to Nicholas G. Cox, Esq. of the Search Room, Public Record Office (letter of 9 October 1975).

[25] *The Index Library. Prerogative Court of Canterbury Wills* IV, 1584–1604 (1910), *sub* 1603.

[26] W.H. Godfrey, A.R. Wagner and H.S. London, *The College of Arms* (London Survey Committee, 1963), p. 196. This reference and the information that there appear to be no examples of Mercury's work in the College of Arms is by courtesy of Dr F.W. Steer, Maltravers Herald Extraordinary (letter of 10 November 1975).

[27] *Memorials of St Margaret's Church, Westminster* . . . ed. A.M. Burke (London, 1914), p. 524.

[28] P.R.O. SP 14/107, no. 82, 104D.

[29] *Memorials*, p. 578 and n. 5.

William Patten himself lived through the affray of February 1601 in the City, when Robert Devereux, the 2nd Earl of Essex, rode along Fleet Street, Ludgate Hill and Cheapside, and was pushed out of the City and down to the river by troops headed by Cecil's elder son Thomas, Lord Burghley. The old rivalries between the Queen's men, William Cecil, 'Sir Spirit', and Leicester, her 'Eyes', were ultimately played out between Robert Devereux and Robert Cecil, the Earl of Leicester's stepson and William's younger boy.

Tom Trotter's escape from Castle Thornton with the keys, leaving sixteen Scots souls inside to defend it since they could not get out, the tumult of Hock-Tuesday, Harry Goldingham, tipsy astride a dolphin twenty-four feet long, and, in 1598, the death in office of William Cecil who had shared so much, belonged to a different century, to a waning age. When we consider the teeming bustle of London under the Tudors, the cheapness of life, the executions of Royal friends and enemies, and the incidence of plague and pestilence, it is quite remarkable that this Tudor Londoner, great only in years, has left us so much of himself and his endeavours during such a glorious and troubled period of English history.

On 2 November 1601 letters of administration of the estate of William Patten, late of the parish of St Bartholomew the Great, close by West Smithfield, were granted to his son, Mercury Patten, by proxy to Edward Willet.[30] For the last of the Tudors, 'the Seaventh of my God', who had been the subject of her subject Patten's intellectual devotions, there was little time left before the Palace of Richmond. Yet it was only just over half a century and three reigns ago, that her father had seen the smoke settle over the Solent and David Googan had laid down his life for Harry Tudor and his England.

[30] P.R.O. Prob. 6/6, 99 verso.

# III

# William Bedell and the Universal Language Movement in Seventeenth-century Ireland

## VIVIAN SALMON

In the course of Gulliver's visit to Laputa, he encountered an institution which was the object of one of Swift's more amusing and good-natured satires—the Grand Academy of Lagado, whose professors communicated, not in speech, but in objects, to which they pointed when they wished to converse. It was argued that since 'Words are only Names for *Things*, it would be more convenient for all Men to carry about them, such *Things* as were necessary to express the particular Business they are to discourse on'. The heavy burdens imposed on the speakers were justified on the grounds that this mode of discourse 'would serve as an universal Language to be understood in all civilized Nations'.[1] The target of Swift's satire was the universal language movement which, beginning in the early seventeenth century, culminated in the year after Swift was born in a magnificent, if misguided achievement—John Wilkins's *An Essay towards a Real Character, and a Philosophical Language* (1668). Laudable as were the aims of the movement, which were to remedy the ambiguity of normal language and to provide a satisfactory form of scientific discourse internationally comprehensible, the means adopted by the language inventors and their excessive ambitions laid them open to ridicule; they believed that it was possible to list and classify every object in the universe, to place it in an ordered arrangement, and to assign it a name in which every syllable would be significant of some quality of the object, or of its place in a hierarchy.

It was not until after the publication of the *Essay* that serious doubts began to be expressed about the feasibility of the project, and then mainly in private;[2] Swift seems to have been the first to express ridicule, and in public. It is generally assumed that his acquaintance

---

[1] Jonathan Swift, *Gulliver's Travels (1726)*. Introduction by H. Williams (Oxford, 1941), pp. 169–70.

[2] Cf. V. Salmon, 'John Wilkins' *Essay*: Critics and continuators', *The Study of Language in Seventeenth-century England* (Amsterdam, 1979), pp. 191–206.

with the universal language movement was through the *Essay*, which was published in London under the ægis of the Royal Society; in fact, he may have had a much closer connection with the movement in his native Ireland. While he was an undergraduate at Trinity College, Dublin, the professor of mathematics, Miles Symner, had been at one time closely involved in sponsoring an early form of universal language created by a friend, John Johnson;[3] just before he graduated a universal language scheme was presented by the Rev. John Keogh to the Dublin Philosophical Society;[4] and there was current in Dublin another such scheme, published there in 1679, of which the sole surviving copy is in the library of the man who presented Swift to the Prebend of Dunlavin in 1700—Archbishop Narcissus Marsh, who owned the *Tractatus de Literis et Lingua Philosophica* composed by a Dublin physician, Nathaniel Chamberlain[5]. Swift's satire on the professors of the Grand Academy may have been aimed, therefore, not only at the English Royal Society and its sponsorship of the *Essay* but also at the universal language schemes devised by contemporaries in Dublin in his undergraduate years.

Much is known already about the history of the universal language movement in England and France,[6] but no account has hitherto been given of its development in Ireland. But many scholars, either born there or resident at the relevant time, were actively engaged in the seventeenth century in creating some form of artificial communication; at first it was simply a written character, called a 'Real' character because its symbols represented *res* 'things' and not words, and like Arabic numerals, could be 'read off' in any language; later, genuine languages were devised, with both written and spoken forms and symbols which denoted the qualities of the objects to which they were assigned—so-called 'iconic' forms. Between the first attempt in the early 1630s to the last known Irish universal language scheme designed in the 1680s, several efforts were made to

---

[3] The fullest account of Symner appears in T. C. Barnard, 'Miles Symner and the new learning in seventeenth-century Ireland', *Journal of the Royal Society of Antiquaries of Ireland,* 102 (1972), pp. 129–42.

[4] R. Gunther, 'Dr. Plot and the correspondence of the Philosophical Society', *Early Science in Oxford*, XII (Oxford, 1939), p. 181.

[5] Cf. V. Salmon, 'Nathaniel Chamberlain', in *Five Hundred Years of Words and Sounds: Studies in the English Language 1200–1700* [for E.J. Dobson] ed. D. Gray and E.G. Stanley (forthcoming).

[6] Cf. J. Knowlson, *Universal Language Schemes in England and France 1600–1800* (Toronto, 1975).

promulgate an artificial mode of communication; but to provide a coherent account is no simple matter because such information as is available is often in the form of casual references in many disparate sources. The most valuable are the two biographies (written by members of his family) of William Bedell, an Englishman who, after graduating from Cambridge in 1588–9, eventually became Provost of Trinity College, Dublin (1627–29) and finally Bishop of Kilmore and Ardagh, dying in 1642 as a result of hardships undergone in the Irish rebellion of the previous year.[7] Another particularly valuable source is the diary, known as *Ephemerides*, kept by Samuel Hartlib; he was the centre of a group of educational and religious reformers who regularly sent him in London information about the progress of their various schemes for the betterment of the world, references to which appear in the diary (denoted below as H followed by the relevant year). Both the manuscript diary and many letters to Hartlib are preserved in Sheffield University, the latter items arranged in bundles labelled by Roman numerals.

Of all the scholars active in Ireland, there is no doubt that the most important is William Bedell; it was he who, in the first place, conceived the idea of creating a universal character, and it is from his initiative that the other projects, directly or indirectly, can be traced. His interest in the improvement of communication may be explained by the circumstances of his own life and experiences, and his active engagement in drawing up a scheme for a character by his own distinguished linguistic abilities. His own experiences brought to his attention problems of two kinds: first, difficulties in communication in daily life between speakers of differing vernaculars; secondly, problems of communication between the clergy, in both religious and domestic affairs, and an illiterate population speaking a different vernacular from their mentors, unable to understand the rituals of the church or to read the sacred books, and even where they shared the language of those preaching the Gospel, to comprehend the words and phrases they used. Bedell met with the first kind of problem when he accompanied Sir Henry Wotton to Venice, in 1607, as his chaplain; he found himself obliged to learn Italian, in which he delivered his sermons, and was asked by his Italian friends to assist them in learning English. To do so, he 'compos'd an English

---

[7] The biographies by his son William and his stepson-in-law Alexander Clogie are printed in E. S. Shuckburgh, *Two Biographies of William Bedell* (Cambridge, 1902), pp. 1–75 and 79–213 respectively. Clogie's papers were used in Gilbert Burnet's *Life* of Bedell (1685).

grammar . . . letting them see our language to be reducible into the bounds of art, and not obscure and barbarous as commonly they accounted it then beyond the seas, but elegant and copious and easy enough'.[8] It did not, however, prove easy enough to learn, as Bedell and his Italian friend, Jasper Despotine, discovered to their cost. When Bedell returned to England, he was accompanied by Despotine, who was a convert to the Protestant religion, and intended to set up in practice as a physician in Suffolk. He found himself in great difficulty through 'his want of the English tongue. But his friend Mr Bedell would not see him suffer for this, but voluntarily took upon him to be his interpreter at any time whensoever any patient should resort unto him'. Even with this assistance, the situation was not a happy one for the immigrant: 'considering his condition being a stranger wanting language, being unfit for humane society and burtensom, as he accounted, to his friend, he was at first even weary of himself (S. 13–14).' Fortunately, his depression lifted as he 'gained upon' the English language, but the experience must have made a deep impression on Bedell.

As Bishop of Kilmore (from 1629) Bedell was confronted with a related problem of communication, but in religious matters. As he wrote to Archbishop Laud shortly after his appointment to the See, 'there are Seven or Eight Ministers in each Diocese of good sufficiency; and (which is no small cause of the continuance of the people in Popery still) *English*, which have not the Tongue of the people . . nor can perform any Divine offices, or converse with them.'[9] Unable to communicate with large numbers in his spiritual care in either English or Latin, Bedell must have felt himself to be in the same situation as Protestant missionaries like John Eliot, the 'Apostle of the Indians', who, emigrating to America at about the same time as Bedell entered on his religious duties in Ireland, decided that it was essential for him to learn the language of the natives, and spent two years in the study of the relevant American Indian language before daring to preach in that tongue.[10] Bedell did likewise; he 'gave himself as earnestly to learn the Irish tongue in Kilmore . . . as he had done formerly to learn the Italian . . . in Venice' (S. 133).

---

[8] Shuckburgh, pp. 3–4. Future references to his work will be made in the text, indicated by the letter S prefixed to the page number.

[9] Burnet, *Life*, pp. 46–7.

[10] On Eliot's linguistic achievements, cf. V. Salmon, *The Works of Francis Lodwick* (London, 1972), pp. 49–51.

Although he found the Irish language, as he informed a friend, learned, exact and difficult,[11] he nevertheless 'made a progress beyond all expectation' (S. 133) and composed an Irish grammar, although he was never able to do more than read and write the language (S. 42).

Even when Protestant congregations were English-speaking, difficulties of communication remained because of the highly rhetorical style adopted by Anglican preachers in the later sixteenth century. John Wilkins's advocacy of a plain style in *Ecclesiastes* (1646) has been seen as foreshadowing the Royal Society's requirement of a simple style for contributions to its *Transaction*, as well as one feature in the evolution of a non-ambiguous lexicon in the *Essay* of 1668;[12] but before this date, Bedell had aimed at the enlightenment of his hearers by using the simplest of language. As his biographers relate: 'his prayer before sermon was . . . ever in the plainest and easiest phrase of the English tongue, according to the capacity of the weakest understanding . . . he never affected tedious prolixity or needless verbosity' (S. 6) and he did not 'seeke to please the eares with a fyled speech and floorish of words' (S. 154). When he eventually directed the translation of the Old Testament into Irish he likewise insisted that it should be in 'the plainest Irish, most understood of the vulgar' (S. 132).

From his personal experience Bedell therefore had every reason to be aware of problems of communication in lay and religious matters, either through the existence of mutually incomprehensible vernaculars or through the use of rhetorical and ambiguous language. Unlike most of his contemporaries, who must have been equally aware of these problems, he tried to find solutions to them, and he was able to do so, at least in part, because he was a brilliant linguist. As a young man, he was 'eminent' in Greek, in Latin 'none did excell him' (S. 82), he had 'no mean skill' (S. 3) in Syriac, Arabic and Hebrew, and when he set out to learn Italian, he was 'suddenly as much master of it as if he had been an Italian born' (S. 82). In Irish, he became competent enough to assist in translating the Old Testament (S. 55–6). Moreover, as his son reports, he 'had this rare faculty, that whatsoever art or language he would set himself to acquire, he would reduce it into a body or method of his own contrivance, and

[11] Tanner MS 72, f. 288.
[12] Cf. R.F. Jones, *The Seventeenth Century* (Stanford, 1951, repr. 1969), p. 78.

of languages usually he would draw up a grammar' (S. 3). The production of grammars was therefore one contribution he made to the improvement of international communication; the translation of important texts a second (S. 82); and a third was the encouragement of fluency in Irish by the intensive training of Trinity College undergraduates destined for the ministry (S. 25, 41). His contribution to the teaching of Irish, including the publication of an Irish-English school primer, or *A.B.C.* (S. 125), is a subject deserving separate study; the present paper is devoted to his quite different attempt to improve international communication by devising a 'Real Character'. The first fruits of this attempt were the 'translation' of a scientific work into the 'Real Character', and there seems to be no evidence that he ever considered such a device as a means of communication in domestic or religious matters.

Occupied as he was with the affairs of his diocese, at a particularly difficult time for the Church in Ireland, he did not, or could not, devise a 'Real Character' single-handed. What he could do was to draw on his experience and abilities as a linguist to provide an outline and model for such an enterprise, and to find someone with the leisure and intelligence to execute it in detail. Fortunately, the right man was available. It was Bedell's policy to encourage his clergy to reside in their parishes, but one of these, named Johnson, was unwilling to do so. Bedell persuaded him to take on the task, urging that the enterprise was entirely feasible since 'Real Characters' already existed for mathematics, geometry, astronomy, and the figures of the Zodiac (S. 109–10). Johnson agreed, and Bedell 'gave him a platform', as his stepson-in-law reported (S. 110)—a phrase which was translated by Gilbert Burnet as 'drew for him a Scheme of the Whole Work'[13]. Burnet also explains that Bedell gave Johnson this task so that he might not be wholly useless to the church, but there is no reference to this motivation in Burnet's source, which was Clogie's account.

This is the last we hear of Bedell's personal involvement in the 'Real Character', but the survival of his ideas was ensured by Johnson's continuing to 'observe'—as Clogie says—the scheme of the work which Bedell drew up. Of Johnson himself Clogie tells us very little, but it is possible to identify him from other sources. Among the Hartlib manuscripts is a letter from Miles Symner to a friend, dated (in a copy in Sloane MS 427 f. 85) 24 October 1648. Symner

[13] Burnet, *Life*, p. 79.

reports that Johnson's manuscript was destroyed by 'the fryars in Athenry' in the Irish rebellion. Three conclusions may be drawn from this remark: first, that since the papers are likely to have been in Johnson's house, he must have lived at Athenry; secondly, that Johnson could not have been of Irish origin, since native Irish Protestant ministers were spared in the rebellion (as was Dennis Sheridan, a friend of Bedell, who was able to rescue his manuscript translation of the Old Testament in Irish (S. 70) ); thirdly, that if Johnson was a clergyman, living in Athenry, he was in all likelihood the incumbent. So it proves; the incumbent was John Johnson, instituted in 1639. He was a Fellow of Trinity College Dublin while Bedell was Provost (1627–9); he took his B.A. in 1618, his M.A. in 1621, and was elected to a Fellowship in 1622.[14] In 1627 he is described as 'bursar' and his signature as a senior Fellow is appended to various letters in 1627–9.[15] While he was an undergraduate complaints were made of the large numbers of students from overseas, at one time twelve from Derbyshire and eight from Cheshire being recorded, out of some sixty to seventy undergraduates.[16] That Johnson was one of these, rather than a Scot, is suggested by a description of him given in a letter from the French scholar Father Mersenne to one of Hartlib's friends, Theodore Haak, in 1640: Mersenne refers to him as an 'Anglois d'Irlande'.[17] It is worth noting that two other men who were scholars at Trinity College in the 1620s were also concerned with the improvement of communication. In the case of one, Thomas Price (later Archbishop of Cashel), Narcissus Marsh relates that it was because Price had been trained by Bedell, and had therefore encouraged the use of Irish in the Church, that Marsh himself tried 'to use all his exertions towards encouraging the Study of Irish among the Scholars of that [i.e. Trinity] College'[18] while he was Provost. The second of these associates of Johnson's was Miles Symner, who was active in promulgating the universal character after Johnson's death.

Johnson, who left Trinity College in 1629 for benefices in Bedell's

[14] G.D. Burtchaell and T.U. Sadleir, *Alumni Dublinenses*, rev. ed. (Dublin, 1935).

[15] J.W. Stubbs, *The History of the University of Dublin* (Dublin, 1889), pp. 55, 390, 393, 395, 402.

[16] Stubbs, p. 42.

[17] *Correspondance du P. Marin Mersenne*, ed. P. Tannery and C. de Waard, XI (Paris, 1970), 417–18.

[18] H. Cotton, *Fasti Ecclesiæ Hiberniæ* (Dublin, 1845), I.92, footnote (a).

other diocese of Ardagh (possibly in order to marry, or under the 'seven-year rule' for Fellows which Bedell had enforced) was extremely well fitted for his new task.[19] Clogie describes him as 'a man of a great reach' (S. 109) [Burnet (p. 78) 'of very quick Parts'], an 'ingenious man' (S. 110 fn.) [Burnet: of 'a great Capacity'], while a recent acquaintance, writing in 1636 to the Duke of Ormonde, describes him as 'the best . . . for judgment and skill in the whole kingdom' and 'a learned and good man'.[20] Personally, as Clogie reports, he had a 'mercuriall wit', while there is a hint at arrogance in the comment, in the letter of 1636, that while Johnson is willing to take pains for the writer, 'he doth not use to do so much for others'. Not only was he conventionally 'learned'—he had great practical ability as well. Clogie reports that he had a 'mechanick' education (S. 110), which Burnet mistakenly interprets as 'mean'; and in recommending him for employment, Ormonde's correspondent describes him as 'an able and expert man for surveying'. Such a technical skill seems an odd accomplishment for a member of the clergy, but that it was not so unusual at the time is suggested by the appointment of the Reverend Miles Symner to the Chair of Mathematics at Trinity College in 1652, for the special purpose of lecturing on surveying.[21] Clogie also reports that Johnson was later employed as an 'engenier' by Lord Deputy Strafford at his 'great and glorious' buildings in Co. Wicklow. Since 'engenier' in the 1630s implied an ability to design and construct military fortifications, it seems probable that Clogie was wrong, and that Johnson's employment was as supervisor of the building operations, an occupation much more appropriate to his experience as bursar.[22] Unfortunately, this engagement delayed the completion of the 'Real Character'; as Hartlib reports in the *Ephemerides* (1639 JJ7): 'He hase been all this while too much taken up with my Lord deputyes businesses.'

Johnson, both 'learned' and 'practical', was ideally qualified to take up Bedell's suggestion, and it is not surprising that, when we have news of his progress, it is that he is busy 'translating' a scientific

---

[19] He may also have had benefices earlier in the 1620s. Cf. R. Loeber, *A Biographical Dictionary of Architects in Ireland 1600–1720* (London, 1981), pp. 62–3.

[20] *Calendar of the Manuscripts of the Marquess of Ormonde* (London, 1902), N.S. I.36–7.

[21] Barnard, 'Miles Symner', p. 130.

[22] Cf. H.G. Leask, 'Early seventeenth-century houses in Ireland', in *Studies in Building History*, ed. E.M. Jope (London, 1961), pp. 244–5.

work into the 'Real Character', which he called *Wit-spell* (S. 110). The work is a botanical treatise which Hartlib describes as 'Jhones Herbarium Angliæ' (H1639 EFI). Neither author nor publication can be identified by the names which Hartlib gives, but there can be little doubt about what he intended. The spelling 'Jhones' is probably for 'Johnson', and the reference to the 'Herbarium' must be to the first publication devoted solely to English flora. This was the *Mercurius Botanicus* of Thomas Johnson, of which the first volume appeared in 1634.[23] There are several reasons why this work might have been an early choice; one was the great importance of botany in an age of herbal medicine; a second reason was a more trivial one—the choice of the *Mercurius* might have been Bedell's suggestion, arising from his own special interests. His son reports that he devoted some of his spare time to 'planting, transplanting, grafting and inoculating, and sometimes digging in his garden' (S.17). Thirdly, there is a slight possibility that Johnson's choice of the *Mercurius* might have been motivated by the fact that its author was a kinsman. Unfortunately, both names are too common to make it possible to establish a relationship with any certainty.

Hartlib reports that Johnson intended to extend his translations to 'other natural domestic [i.e. indigenous] things' (H1639 EFI), but he tells us nothing directly about his method. It seems that he used non-alphabetic symbols, which Mersenne refers to as 'hieroglyphics',[24] and which had to be engraved on copper plates.[25] He invented no symbols for proper names, for which presumably he must have devised (as did John Wilkins) an internationally comprehensible phonetic alphabet, and very oddly, he provided no symbols for the 'species of herbs' (H1640 DE3). Perhaps he devised a symbol for the genus, followed by a number referring to a list of species; at all events, he reported no difficulty with his scheme except for the 'syncategoremata' (S. 110), i.e. the grammatical 'form' words such as conjunctions and prepositions. In a letter to a friend in 1640 Hartlib reports that although Descartes himself is engaged on a universal language, Johnson 'is preferred before all the rest as having studied

[23] Cf. H.W. Kew and H.E. Powell, *Thomas Johnson* (London, 1932), p. 136. C. Webster, *The Great Instauration* (London, 1975), p. 468 describes the work as representing 'a new level of sophistication in English botany'.
[24] *Correspondance*, XI. 417–18.
[25] Cf. M.M. Slaughter, *Universal Languages and Scientific Taxonomy in the Seventeenth Century* (Cambridge, 1982), p. 111. Slaughter also prints many of Hartlib's references to Johnson on pp. 235–6, footnotes 31–2.

the subject these many years over & over, in soe much that at this very Instant hee is contriving how to publish & discover the whole invention & mysterie that all the World may have a reall benefit of it'.[26]

By 1640 only a few sheets of the 'Real Character' had been printed, and Johnson is reported as needing another two years to complete it (H1640 BC8). But in October 1641 the Irish rebellion broke out, and Johnson was 'despoiled of all his goods . . . and chattels'.[27] In particular, as Symner reports, the friars of Athenry tore up his manuscript 'for heresy', destroyed the printed sheets and gave the copper plates away for 'tinkers to stop kettles w$^{th}$'. Johnson, his wife Julian and their ten children took refuge on an island in the neighbouring county of Offaly, but at Christmas Johnson and his eldest son were killed by the rebels. His wife and the remaining children escaped to Dublin, where they were living on charity, and in great hardship, when in 1643 Julian Johnson gave this account of their fate.[28] All that remained of *Wit-spell* was 'the first unpolished coppy' which came into the possession of Miles Symner and which he hoped might be published, claiming that he ought to be 'at the birth of it' because he was 'best acquainted w$^{th}$it'.[29] In fact, he seems to have completed Johnson's work himself, since in the previous year Haak wrote to Mersenne, telling him that they were awaiting the arrival of someone from Ireland who 'has brought to a conclusion . . . the efforts of more than twenty years of a . . . skilful man of that kingdom (died 3 or 4 years ago) to write in a way that the message may be read at once in all languages'.[30] This was presumably Symner, who is reported again in 1649 as offering to bring the 'Real Character' to England (H1649 AB8); this was eventually brought, not by Symner, now busy with Cromwell's forces in Ireland, but by Johnson's widow (H1650 KL1). Hartlib records that one 'Mr. French . . . very mathematical and of strong imaginations' would be a fit person to revise it (H1650 HJ8), but others were disappointed. A 'Dr. Fuller' (who seems to be the Thomas Fuller who was appointed to the See of Ardfert in 1641, thereafter taking refuge from the rebellion in London and Oxford) is reported to believe that this first draft is far

---

[26]  Hartlib MSS, VII, 43.
[27]  M. Hickson, *Ireland in the Seventeenth Century* (London, 1884), II.14.
[28]  ibid., pp. 14–15.
[29]  Sloane MS 427, f. 85 r. Also in Hartlib MSS XLVII.6.
[30]  Knowlson, *Universal Language Schemes*, pp. 53–4.

inferior to 'his later contrivances' (H1650 KL1), and Fuller and two others were now setting to work on their own system. As for *Wit-spell*, its last known home was with a friend of Symner's, Anthony Morgan, who moved to Ireland with Cromwell's army but kept up his interest in universal language, being one of those who gave financial help to George Dalgarno to publish his *Ars Signorum* in 1662.[31]

In his letter of 1648 Symner expressed the hope that, by finishing and publishing Johnson's attempt at 'Real Character', he would 'sett other men on work'. This certainly seems to have been the case with Fuller and his colleagues, and possibly even one of the reasons why there was so much interest in the subject in Oxford after 1650, the date of Hartlib's report about Fuller. In 1654 Seth Ward, Professor of Astronomy, published an account of a universal language in which he had been engaged,[32] and several other scholars became involved in discussions which were to lead eventually to the publication of Wilkins's *Essay* in 1668.[33] Among them were William Petty, Professor of Anatomy, until he left for Ireland in 1653, and possibly Narcissus Marsh, who, graduating in 1657–8, became chaplain to Seth Ward when he was appointed to the see of Exeter. Yet another Oxford scholar of the 1650s to move to Ireland, and who was interested in universal language projects, was Robert Wood of Lincoln College; Hartlib consulted him in 1657 for his views on the universal language currently under construction by George Dalgarno,[34] and Wood later contributed money to assist its publication.

Of these scholars, only Petty remained actively involved in designing a universal language when he settled in Dublin, in so far as he wrote papers associated with the topic in 1685 and 1686;[35] Petty's most specific involvement with universal language must have been as President of the Dublin Philosophical Society when John Keogh's work was presented. Keogh, a graduate of Trinity College in 1678, was a noted mathematician and linguist and, according to his son,

[31] Barnard, 'Miles Symner', p. 142, footnote 93.
[32] *Vindiciæ Academiarum* (Oxford, 1654), pp. 20–2.
[33] Cf. V. Salmon, 'The evolution of Dalgarno's *Ars Signorum*', *The Study of Language*, pp. 157–75.
[34] Salmon, p. 163.
[35] *The Dictionary of Sensible Words* (1685) and *The Explication of 12 Theological Words* (1686), printed in *The Petty Papers*, ed. Marquis of Lansdowne (London, 1927), I.150–1, 162–6.

'there was hardly any Branch of Learning, from the Alphabet to the Oriental Languages, but he was acquainted with'.[36] In December 1685 'A Large discourse concerning the formation of Letters and an Universall Character was presented from Mr. J. Keagh [sic], some part thereof was read'.[37] The remainder was adjourned, but no further discussion is recorded in the minutes of the Society.

Swift may possibly have heard of this apparent failure—due perhaps to general realization by the end of the century that the whole enterprise, however idealistic, was a sheer absurdity. What is more likely is that Swift actually read a small tract on universal language which was printed in Dublin in 1679. This was the *Tractatus de Literis et Lingua Philosophica* by the English physician, Nathaniel Chamberlain, who appears to have been practising in Dublin at about that time, and who acknowledges in the dedication the assistance he has received from William Hill. Hill, a distinguished philologist, had been appointed headmaster of the grammar school in Dublin in 1656, though after the Restoration he had retired to a living in Finglas.[38] Chamberlain relates how Hill had read his draft and made detailed improvements, although he advised the author to complete his work before publishing so that a large number of others would not try to complete it independently of one another, the result being total confusion. If Hill knew of the aftermath of *Wit-spell*, this is no doubt exactly the advice he would have given. But Chamberlain, by now no longer a young man (he had graduated from Oxford in 1636), decided not to wait. His book, though short, was quite comprehensive, including a discussion of orthography, phonology, grammar and the construction of an ordered lexicon. A description of its contents has been given elsewhere,[39] and all that need be said is that all trace of it disappeared until recently (except as one of Wing's 'Ghosts')[40] when a search was instituted in Dublin and a copy found in Narcissus Marsh's library.

Bedell's quest for a better means of communication proved an inspiration for many later scholars in both Ireland and England. All, to judge from the evidence of contemporaries, were intelligent and

---

[36] J. Keogh, *A Vindication of the Antiquities of Ireland* (Dublin, 1748), p. 146.

[37] R. Gunther, 'The correspondence of Dr. Plot', p. 181. Cf. K.T. Hoppen, *The Common Scientist in the Seventeenth Century* (London, 1970), p. 155.

[38] C. Webster, *The Great Instauration*, p. 228 and T.C. Barnard, *Cromwellian Ireland* (London, 1975), pp. 195–7.

[39] V. Salmon, 'Nathaniel Chamberlain' (cf. note 5 above).

[40] D. Wing, *A Gallery of Ghosts* (New York, 1967), p. 44.

learned; some, like Keogh and Hill, were also brilliant linguists; others, like Johnson and Symner, highly accomplished in practical skills. It is sad indeed that the ideals—unattainable though they may have been—of men such as these should be remembered as the subject of Swift's mockery, rather than his admiration.

I am greatly indebted to Dr T.C. Barnard for a personal communication about an item in the Hartlib MSS and the reference cited in footnote 19. I am also very grateful to Dr C. Webster for information on other Hartlib MSS, especially on that cited in footnote 26.

## IV

# 'A True Representation': Speech in the Novels of Thomas Hardy

## RAYMOND CHAPMAN

The *Athenaeum* review of *The Return of the Native* was generally unfavourable. There was, however, one particular criticism which distressed Hardy enough to move him to write a reply. The reviewer objected to the unnatural quality of the dialogue: 'People talk as no people ever talked before, or perhaps we should say as no people ever talk now.' The speech of the rustic characters came in for the strongest objection: 'The language of his peasants may be Elizabethan, but it can hardly be Victorian.'[1] Criticism was directed against lexis and syntax rather than phonic representation, but Hardy's defence shows his own major concern in the matter of dialect:

> An author may be said to fairly convey the spirit of intelligent peasant talk if he retains the idiom, compass, and characteristic expressions, although he may not encumber the page with obsolete pronunciations of the purely English words, and with mispronunciations of those derived from Latin and Greek. In the printing of standard speech hardly any phonetic principle at all is observed; and if a writer attempts to exhibit on paper the precise accents of a rustic speaker he disturbs the proper balance of a true representation by unduly insisting upon the grotesque element; thus directing attention to a point of inferior interest, and diverting it from the speaker's meaning.[2]

The charge of making his peasants too refined and sophisticated in their speech was not a new experience for Hardy. In reviewing *Far From the Madding Crowd*, Andrew Lang had observed, 'Shepherds may talk in this way: we hope not.'[3] The critic in the *Saturday Review* had a similar reaction: 'We feel either that we have misjudged the

---

[1] *Athenaeum* 1878 (2), p. 654.
[2] *Athenaeum*, p. 688.
[3] *Academy* 1875, vii, p. 9.

unenfranchised agricultural classes, or that Mr Hardy has put his own thoughts and words into their mouths' (1875, xxix, 57–8). Even earlier, Hardy had been criticized for making the rustics in *Under the Greenwood Tree* 'express themselves in the author's manner of thought, rather than in their own'.[4] Hardy was all his life notoriously sensitive to adverse criticism. His response to the *Athenaeum* review shows that he was less troubled by the charge of stilted and over-elevated dialogue than by any suggestion that his rendering of peasant speech was not accurate upon the ear. This was not the main point at issue, although it arose later in the presentation of Farfrae in *The Mayor of Casterbridge*. As late as 1912 when he wrote a preface for the 'Wessex' edition of this novel, Hardy was repeating his defence of 1878:

> Objections have been raised to the Scotch language of Mr. Farfrae . . . one of his fellow-countrymen went so far as to declare that men beyond the Tweed did not and never could say 'warrld', 'cannet', 'advairrtisment', and so on. As this gentleman's pronunciation in correcting me seemed to my Southron ear an exact repetition of what my spelling implied, I was not struck with the truth of his remark, and somehow we did not get any forwarder in the matter. It must be remembered that the Scotchman of the tale is represented not as he would appear to other Scotchmen, but as he would appear to people of outer regions. Moreover, no attempt is made herein to reproduce his entire pronunciation phonetically, any more than that of the Wessex speakers.

A hostile reader could perhaps accuse Hardy of indifference or incompetence in the accurate presentation of unusual speech. In fact, he was much concerned about a problem which went deeper than the reviewers' objections to unconvincing idiom and which is seldom fully solved by writers of fictional dialogue. The question of dialect in literature had become more apparent to Victorian writers than to their predecessors. Fielding, Smollett, and above all Scott, had created dialect-speaking characters and tried to present the sound of their speech through visible signs. The extent of the issue, and the need for greater precision, increased both with the growing popularity of the novel and with the new mobility which made readers familiar with speakers from regions other than their own. Novelists

---

[4] *Saturday Review* 1872, xxxiv, p. 417.

were looking more seriously at the difficulties of presenting speech-sounds through the written language.

Those difficulties remain to this day, and may be very briefly summarized. The basic problem is a language with twenty-six letters in its written realization and over forty phonemes in the standard or 'received' type of its spoken realization—with a number more in dialects and idiophones. English spelling has developed along lines which were basically phonemic but which have diverged from any consistent relationship. In addition to the discrepancy between letters and phonemes, such correspondence as is possible often relates to earlier and obsolete pronunciation. In ordinary circumstances we switch happily enough from one realization to the other, and can read aloud or write notes of a speech without difficulty. To convey an accurate idea of what is meant to be heard in speech is another matter. There are very few markers to show the vital elements of stress and intonation, none to show pitch or pace: very little, in fact, to put back into writing the features which are lost in the visual code. The distinctive quality of individual voices cannot be shown by a transcription in the common alphabet.

The remedies available to imaginative writers are also few and simple to enumerate, though capable of complexity in their application. The writer can use direct mention and description of what is heard, relying on the reader's experience of speech to translate it into a silent auditory experience. He can enhance the effect by metaphor, simile or synaesthesia—expressing one sensory perception in terms of another, as when we describe a voice as 'cold', 'hard', or 'bitter'. He can use the limited resources of punctuation and typography, relying on marks of interrogation and exclamation to suggest the appropriate intonations, using italics or capital letters for loud and emphatic speech. In the matter of dialect particularly, it is possible to use deviant spelling, supplemented by such things as apostrophes to show omitted sounds, in the hope that any relationship which exists between normal spelling and standard speech will guide the reader to interpret the deviance.

This last is the most popular method of showing unusual speech in fictional dialogue. It is subject to the hazard of defeating its own communicative purpose by a multiplicity of unfamiliar signals. As one writer on dialect in the novel has observed: 'Dialogue can, frankly, be a bore; apostrophes and misspellings are as difficult to a reader's eye as a ploughed field to his boots.'[5] This was the danger in

---

[5] Phyllis Bentley, *The English Regional Novel* (London, 1941), p. 43.

Hardy's mind when he feared an excess of the 'grotesque element' in writing dialect. He had examples to give him warning, such as the speeches of Joseph in *Wuthering Heights* and the dialect poems of Tennyson and William Barnes. Popular literature also showed the hazards; whether the purpose of dialect was radical protest or comic parody, it was too easy to produce what one later Victorian commentator described as 'a perplexing, eye-wearying, phonetic puzzle'.[6]

Hardy had no wish to puzzle his readers; he might well have reflected that he seemed to give adequate reason for adverse criticism without that. He had some cause for annoyance when, in 1881, he was instanced as the kind of writer whose 'thorough knowledge of the dialectical peculiarities of certain districts has tempted them to write whole conversations which are, to the ordinary reader, nothing but a series of linguistic puzzles'. In a letter published in the *Spectator* on 15 October that year he explained and defended his own practice with an intelligent sense of the besetting problem:

> So much has my practice been the reverse of this (as a glance at my novels will show), that I have been reproved for too freely translating dialect-English into readable English, by those of your contemporaries who attach more importance to the publication of local niceties of speech than I do. The rule of scrupulously preserving the local idiom, together with the words which have no synonym among those in general use, while printing in the ordinary way those expressions which are but a modified articulation of words in use elsewhere, is the rule I usually follow; and it is, I believe, generally recognised as the best, where every such rule must of necessity be a compromise, more or less unsatisfactory to lovers of form.[7]

Together with the desire for clarity, Hardy also believed that elaborately deviant presentation of dialect made the novel in which it occurred too localized and strange, with loss of the universality which serious literature should offer. He was concerned that 'Wessex' should be more than just a region of England with charac-

---

[6] E. J. Milliken cited in W. Matthews, *Cockney Past and Present* (London, 1959), p. 160.

[7] This letter was evoked by a review which had appeared in the *Spectator* a week before, discussing a paper on 'George Eliot's use of dialect', which coupled Hardy with George Macdonald; see Harold Orel, *Thomas Hardy's Personal Writings* (London, 1967), pp. 92f.

teristics peculiar to itself. In the general preface to the 1912 edition of
his work he defended his geographical limitations as those which
were not circumstantial but 'he forced them upon himself from
judgement':

> It has sometimes been conceived of novels that evolve their action
> on a circumscribed scene—as do many (though not all) of these—
> that they cannot be so inclusive in their exhibition of human
> nature as novels wherein the scenes cover large extents of country
> . . . I am not concerned to argue this point further than to suggest
> that the conception is an untrue one in respect of the elementary
> passions.

Much earlier, in 1888, he had been dismissive of novels rooted too
much in particularity; 'with absolute accuracy as to idiom, expletive,
slang . . . in aiming at the trivial and the ephemeral they have almost
surely missed better things'.[8]

Hardy thus experienced a certain tension in his imaginative world.
His love and intimate knowledge of his native Dorset and its dialect
must not be allowed to divert the effect of his fiction from universal
reference and his belief in the common lot of all humanity. Speech in
the novel must be distinctive and convincing, but not so quaint or
remote as to dehumanize the speaker. The Dorset poetry of William
Barnes was a warning of possible danger. Hardy deeply respected
Barnes as a man and as a poet; he wrote his obituary, edited a
selection of his work in 1908, and quoted him in his own text (JO
274).[9] Yet the elaborate devices used by Barnes to represent dialect,
with extremely deviant spelling and an extensive use of the diaeresis,
could be a barrier to full appreciation. In his preface to the 1908
selection, Hardy worried that 'lovers of poetry who are but imper-
fectly acquainted with his vocabulary and idiom . . . are liable to
mistake their author on the very threshold'. Yet this was not the
worst:

> For some reason or none, many persons suppose that when

[8] 'The Profitable Reading of Fiction' published in the New York *Forum*,
March 1888; reprinted in Orel, *Personal Writings*, p. 119.

[9] Figures in parentheses after quotations refer to pages in the Macmillan
'Library' edition of the novels (London, 1949 et seqq.); DR: *Desperate Reme-
dies*; HE: *The Hand of Ethelberta*; JO: *Jude the Obscure*; MC: *The Mayor of
Casterbridge*; RN: *The Return of the Native*; TD: *Tess of the D'Urbervilles*; TM:
*The Trumpet Major*; UG: *Under the Greenwood Tree*.

anything is penned in the tongue of the country-side, the primary intent is burlesque or ridicule, and this especially if the speech be one in which the sibilant has the rough sound, and is expressed by Z.

Hardy was aware of the comic association of south-western speech, dating back to the Elizabethan conventional 'stage southern' of the type shown in Edgar's simulated peasant speech (*King Lear* IV, vi). He returned to the point in a further preface to a selection of Barnes's poetry in 1918, with the same argument that he had used in replying to the *Athenaeum* review just forty years earlier:

> As long as the spelling of standard English is other than phonetic it is not obvious why that of the old Wessex language should be phonetic, except in a pronouncing dictionary. We have however to deal with Barnes's verse as he chose to write it, merely premising that his aim in the exact literation of Dorset words is not necessarily to exhibit humour and grotesqueness.

This was the fear which made Hardy unwilling to enter into an elaborate representation of dialect. He valued Dorset speech too much to expose it to the popular response evoked by the kind of signals used by Barnes. For him, the very sounds which would suggest the comic rustic, or 'the pitiable picture known as Hodge'[10] were beautiful, as they were in the mouth of Tess:

> The dialect was on her tongue to some extent, despite the village school: the characteristic of that dialect for this district being the voicing approximately rendered by the syllable UR, probably as rich an utterance as any to be found in human speech. (TD 13)

In addition to this concern for the positive quality of dialect, he had that gift which can best be described as a 'good ear' and which enables a writer to convey auditory experience through the visual signals of writing and awake a more than conventional response in the reader. To do this with the minimum of distraction and the avoidance of comic associations was his aim in presenting fictional dialogue.

A richer talent for exaggerated deviant spelling than appears generally in the novels is shown in some of his private writing. He

---

[10] 'The Dorsetshire Labourer', *Longman's Magazine*, July, 1883, p. 252.

could write to his sister, when he had a bad cold, of a 'cowdid by head' and he was prepared to give cockney speech the treatment which seemed unsuitable for the Dorset dialect. Thus he reproduced the words of a London bus conductor on the vagaries of women cyclists:

> Oh, nao; their sex pertects them. We dares not drive over them wotever they do; & they do jist wot they likes. 'Tis their sex, yer see; & its wot I coll takin' a mean adventage.[11]

Dialect in the novels is given more sparing use of visual signalling. Sometimes only a dialect word suggests the whole tone of a speech: 'And what ghastly gallicrow might the poor fellow have been like?' (RN 25). Deviant spelling of a standard word has the same effect; omission of letters also shows elided pronunciation: 'Mr. Clare has gone hwome to Emminster to spend a few days wi' his kinsfolk' (TD 200). The spelling *hwome* for 'home' was a favourite with William Barnes, who was not content to let it stand as an isolated example. There is gradation in the presentation of dialect, 'lower' characters showing more deviant features. Thus a minor character like the staylace vendor in *The Mayor of Casterbridge* has substandard syntax, dialect words, deviant and elided spellings of regular words:

> I glory in the woman's sperrit. I'd ha' done it myself—od send if I wouldn't, if a husband had behaved so to me! I'd go, and 'a might call, and call, till his keacorn was raw; but I'd never come back— no, not till the great trumpet, would I! (MC 14)

It is an advantage of Hardy's method that the broad dialect can be distinguished from the less broad, while the speech remains intelligible. While a reader who has found the key to Barnes's poems may 'hear' the Dorset accents more precisely, Hardy is successful in maintaining the easy flow of conversation and the distinctions of character which the novel requires. Degrees of relative education and social position are shown through the comparative use of dialect. Thus the first appearance of Jack Durbeyfield is marked by his use of forms like 'Good night t'ee', 'I zaid', 'I be plain Jack Durbeyfield the haggler', in contrast to the parson's standard replies (TD 3). So the language of Crick—'Howsomever, these gam'sters do certainly

---

[11] *The Collected Letters of Thomas Hardy*, ed. R.L. Purdy and M. Millgate (Oxford, 1978), II. 193 (8 May 1898).

keep back their milk to-day'—foregrounds the appearance of Angel Clare among the milkers, when his first remark is made in standard form (TD 141). At the same time, the contrast is not so great as to make the dairyman seem merely comic and of a different grade of humanity, or to stretch the reader's belief in the possibility of a reasonable conversation between the participants.

Throughout his career as a novelist, Hardy was acutely aware of the changes taking place in his native county. In his lifetime its rural parts moved from primitive isolation to a full incorporation into the life of a prosperous southern England. The dialect itself became less marked with the growth of compulsory education, a change which Hardy regarded as something of a loss in respect of a noble form of language. A visitor to a Dorset cottage in 1883 might find that the children 'would occasionally make a sad hash of their talk':

> Having attended the National School they would mix the printed tongue as taught therein with the unwritten, dying, Wessex English that they had learnt of their parents, the result of this transitional state of theirs being a composite language without rule or harmony.[12]

A few years later this sentiment finds expression in fiction:

> Mrs Durbeyfield habitually spoke the dialect; her daughter, who had passed the Sixth Standard in the National School under a London-trained mistress, spoke two languages; the dialect at home, more or less; ordinary English abroad and to persons of quality. (TD 21)

This, the text of the 1912 edition, shows an interesting change from the *Graphic* version of 1891, in which the words after *mistress* are 'used it only when excited by joy, surprise, or grief'—a more effective qualification both psychologically and in terms of how Tess speaks in different parts of the novel. The Victorian convention of making virtuous and sympathetic characters in novels speak in standard English (Oliver Twist, Lizzie Hexam) should also be remembered in this connection.

Apart from the encroachments of education, dialect is seen as a potent social marker and sometimes as divisive. It is eschewed by those who aspire to gentility, or at least attempts are made to

---

[12] 'The Dorsetshire Labourer', p. 253.

eradicate it from the children. It is related that Hardy's mother discouraged his use of dialect speech when he was a child.[13] His father was of no great social pretension but held some status in relation to those around him as a small employer of labour. So Henchard, himself an uneducated speaker, is enraged by Elizabeth-Jane's request to 'bide where you be':

> 'Bide where you be', he echoes sharply. 'Good God, are you only fit to carry wash to a pig-trough, that ye use such words as those?' (MC 148)

A little later, her use of the word 'leery' evokes the response, 'One would think you worked upon a farm!' (MC 155). However, Hardy's view of the social attitude to dialect changed by the beginning of the next century. In an address given in 1908 he said:

> In former times an unfamiliar accent was immediately noted as quaint and odd, even a feature of ridicule in novels, memoirs and conversations of the date. So that while it was the aim of every provincial from the squire to the rustic, to get rid of his local articulation at the earliest moment, he now seems rather to pride himself on retaining it, being, in fact, virtually encouraged to do so.[14]

It may have been so, but by that time Hardy had given up the struggle with dialect and other demands of the novel.

While he was still actively engaged in the craft of fiction, his use of dialect had many roles in addition to the placing of social rank and aspiration. It is frequently employed, often in a broad form, to establish the presence of a new minor character who has a useful but not long-lasting part to play in the action. Such characters need to be quickly identified, given a distinctive voice and kept apart from the idiom of characters who are being more fully developed. They are in some ways like the servants and messengers of Elizabethan drama; in both instances it is the work of a master if they can be given brief credibility. Often the character is in fact a servant, a comfort which was not at that time confined to the rich. Such a speaker can be established by a little substandard syntax and one or two spellings

---

[13] C.J. Weber, *Hardy of Wessex* (New York, 1940), pp. 19f.
[14] *The Society of Dorset Men in London* (Yearbook 1908–09): reprinted in Orel, *Personal Writings*, p. 218.

which suggest dialect pronunciations: 'If business don't drag him out pleasure'll never tempt en, is more like our nater in these parts, sir' (HE 31).

Other characters who make brief appearances have a Shakespearian function of unwitting necessity within the plot or of commentary which means more to the reader than it does to those who utter it. These too are often given dialect markers which are broad enough to distinguish them from the standard speakers in the situation but not so extreme as to make them seem absurd or unreal. Such is the captain of the paddle-steamer who waits for Edward Springrove to board while he and Cytherea believe the distant figure to be her brother Owen:

> Since 'tis her brother, and she's all alone, 'tis only nater to wait a minute, now he's in sight. Suppose, now, you were a young woman, as might be, and had a brother, like this one, and you stood of an evening upon this here wild lonely shore, like her, why you'd want us to wait, too, wouldn't you, sir? I think you would. (DR 29)

In the same novel, Crickett the parish clerk comments in chorus-like fashion on Miss Aldclyffe:

> 'Tis a temper she have . . . though I be a servant of the Church that say it. But she isn't goen to flee in a passion this time. (DR 140)

A more sinister comment is made by the pig-killer Challow in his single appearance just after Jude has killed the pig and his estrangement from Arabella has begun:

> Well done, young married volk! I couldn't have carried it out much better myself, cuss me if I could! (JO 76)

Something more reminiscent of the collective chorus of classical drama is provided by the rustics who pass their observations on life through groups without detailed differentiation. The 'rustic chorus' of *Under the Greenwood Tree* has often been noticed, with its gnomic utterances such as, 'Shall anything saucier be found than united 'ooman?' and the favourable judgement on the clergyman who 'never troubled us wi' a visit from year's end to year's end' (UG 41, 71). An even more collective function is performed by the crowd which greets the arrival of a royal party to review the troops:

There's King Jarge! That's Queen Sharlett! Princess 'Lizabeth!
Princess Sophiar and Meelyer! (TM 105)

The strength of Hardy's use of dialect lies in the sure touch with
which it is made to work within the needs of the fictional situation.
The reader's silent ear becomes attuned to the pattern and learns to
pick up the slight indications of Dorset speech without the jolt to
smooth reading which can be caused by extreme attempts at phonetic representation. Hardy seldom moved from the type of substandard speech which he knew intimately. His creation of Farfrae in
*The Mayor of Casterbridge* is a rare attempt to depict a speaker from a
different region. Farfrae's Scots voice confirms the effect of strange-
ness and of menace to the old order which is suggested by his name
and by his appearance as a comer from distant parts. Hardy's reaction
to criticism of his written speech has already been quoted, with the
same defence that he had used for his representations of Dorset
dialect. It is true that he does not create a very imaginative system of
signals, being content largely with the repeated letter *r* to suggest the
lingual rolled sound characteristic of Scots speech in life and in
fiction, supplemented by a few deviant spellings to show non-
standard vowel sounds. This is in accordance with his regular practice and allows us to identify Farfrae as different from the local
speakers while preserving him as a serious and credible character.
The achievement of this end is accomplished with some skill. It
would have been easy to introduce him with a flow of speech marked
plainly as Scots. In fact his first appearance elicits only a pair of
sentences, with no deviant indicators except the one form *ye* for *you*.
However, attention is drawn to him through the perception of
another character:

Elizabeth-Jane had seen his movements and heard the words,
which attracted her both by their subject and by their accent—a
strange one for those parts. It was quaint and northerly. (MC 43)

A few pages later a waiter makes the more explicit comment, 'He
was a Scotchman seemingly' (MC 45). By the time Farfrae is given an
extended speech we are prepared to 'hear' him as a Scot and to accept
the fairly conventional indicators of his accent:

My name is Donald Farfrae. It is true I am in the corren trade—but
I have replied to no advairrtisment, and arranged to see no one. I

am on my way to Bristol—from there to the other side of the warrld, to try my fortune in the great wheat-growing districts of the West! (MC 52)

A well-known instance in *Jude the Obscure* illustrates Hardy's acute awareness of spoken forms which seemed unusual, and his desire to record them as part of the presentation of character. Phillotson calls his wife: ' "Soo!" he said (this being the way in which he pronounced her name)' (JO 265). The single word plays its small part in building up Phillotson as an individual with his educated but idiophonic speech and perhaps indicates another minor factor in Sue's growing distaste for him as a husband. For the modern reader, it has the extra-textual function of showing the pronunciation which was normative for Hardy; most present-day speakers, certainly those of the younger generation, pronounce the name 'Sue' as [su:] rather than [sju:].

Dialect and idiophonic pronunciation play an important part in Hardy's work, as they do in the dialogue of many novels. His sensitivity to speech and his concern to reach the reader's 'ear' is shown in other ways as well. Commentary on the tone and quality of speech, with or without dialect features, is frequent and imaginative in his fiction. Voice-quality is familiar to everyone but is difficult to describe and measure with scientific accuracy. We readily distinguish our acquaintances by the sounds of their voices, even when several of them may seem to us to speak with the same 'accent' or to have no markedly different features of pronunciation. Hardy often takes care to suggest, by description or analogy, how a character speaks apart from the representation of shared dialect. His great love of music—he once said that he preferred concerts to plays[15]—is a fruitful source of imagery. Eustacia's voice sounds 'somewhat more juvenile and fluty than Charley's' (RN 153) and the same instrumental quality strikes the ear of Angel Clare when he first hears Tess speak—'What a fluty voice one of those milkmaids has! I suppose it is the new one' (TD 154).

Music also supplies language for temporary qualities of voice, especially under the stress of emotion:

'What have I done, then? I am sure I thought we two—' The *tremolo* in her voice causes her to break off. (JO 245)

---

[15] Michael Millgate, *Thomas Hardy: a Biography* (Oxford, 1982), p. 448.

'Ay—and I did sing there—I did—But, Miss Newson'—and Donald's voice musically undulated between two semitones, as it always did when he became earnest—'it's well you feel a song for a few minutes, and your eyes they get quite tearful; but you finish it, and for all you felt you don't mind it or think of it again for a long while.' (MC 108)

Perhaps the most splendid and effective use of musical analogy in a single phrase is the description of how Tess reads the end of the baptismal service for her baby:

Then their sister, with much augmented confidence in the efficacy of the sacrament, poured forth from the bottom of her heart the thanksgiving that follows, uttering it boldly and triumphantly in the stopt-diapason note which her voice acquired when her heart was in her speech, and which will never be forgotten by those who knew her. (TD 120)

Other ways of suggesting voice-quality abound in the novels, too many to attempt more than a briefly illustrative selection here. The alert reader will discern a great many pointers, both to a character's regular type of speech and to temporary tonal quality. It may be done by a simple but effective epithet—'a thin jibbering voice was heard to reply' (RN 26) or by the language of synaesthesia—'a dry, small, repressed voice' (TM 347). A collective tone can evoke a rustic simile—'the pupils were still in school, humming small, like a swarm of gnats' (JO 241). The effect of the immediate situation may also be expressed laconically: ' "Nine," said she, in a heart-swollen tone' (RN 226), either thus directly or by the comment of another character—'Cytherea, why do you say "It would", so entirely in the tone of abstract supposition?' (DR 261). Indeed, the effect of speech on a listener within the story can be highly effective, as in the child's reaction to Mrs Yeobright in her exhaustion:

How funny you draw your breath—like a lamb when you drive him till he's nearly done for. Do you always draw your breath like that? (RN 341)

Features of speech which are generally shared but which impart significance or implication to particular utterances are also carefully depicted. Hardy gives much attention in his fictional dialogue to the prosodic area of spoken language, to stress, intonation, pace, and other non-phonemic qualities. The importance of contrastive stress is well shown when Clym Yeobright, speaking of Eustacia, says, 'and by the assistance of a wife like her', drawing forth his mother's exclamation, 'O, Clym!' and the narrator's explanation, 'Yeobright had enunciated the word "her" with a fervour which, in conversation with a mother, was absurdly indiscreet' (RN 227). Pause and broken intonation can say much more than the words spoken. When Angel watches the milkmaids and remarks to Tess, 'Our tremulous lives are so different from theirs, are they not?', he receives a reply which tells not only the immediate reaction but also a suggestion of coming events:

> 'There are very few women's lives that are not—tremulous,' Tess replied, pausing over the new word as if it impressed her. (TD 235)

The situational reference of apparently simple words can be heightened by brief comment such as 'with a strangely accelerated speech' (HE 155).

Physical or emotional causes can change the actual sounds and enunciation of speech, sometimes making the speaker lose control of the normal prosodic features. Hardy is much concerned with the effect of such changes, which often play a part in a character's destiny. Drunken speech is shown by hesitation and oddly-placed pauses rather than by the more conventional slurring of consonants. For example, the drunken postman who enables Manston to gain possession of a vital letter: 'As—one of Majesty's servants—care—Majesty's mails—duty—put letters—own hands' (DR 361); and Tess's father 'singing in a slow recitative':

> I've-got-a-gr't-family-vault-at-Kingsbere—and   knighted-fore-fathers-in-lead-coffins-there! (TD 13)

Later, Hardy uses repeated vowel letters to suggest the distortion of speech by children crying, as Tess's brother and sisters urge her, unwittingly, towards the disaster of her meeting with Alec:

> 'Tess won't go—o—o and be made a la—a—dy of!—no, she says she wo—o—on't!' they wailed, with square mouths. (TD 54)

Adult crying is shown by less radical breaks in initial consonants—

'He can't, he c–can't be s–so cruel' (DR 118). The unformed lisp of a very small child is shown through deviant spelling—'Idd it cold inthide te hole?' (UG 13). The effect of physical stress may be purely humorous, as when the shouted commands of the inexperienced sergeant who has 'only been in the army three weeks' result in unnatural pauses and a ludicrous prolongation of syllable:

> 'Tention! To the right—left wheel, I mean—no, no, right wheel. Mar—r—r—rch! (TM 203)

Finally, Hardy's treatment of paralinguistic sounds is worthy of attention. A good deal of human communication as well as personal relief of feeling consists not of phonemes organized into words but of laughter, sighs, groans, sharp expirations, and so on. Novelists take account of these, incorporating them into the text by referential mention, description, or imaginative visual representation. Hardy is particularly strong with regard to the choice and arrangement of letters which can suggest sounds that are not themselves semantic words. For example, he often uses the conventional 'ha, ha' signal for laughter. This can be extended without inhibition, to show notably prolonged laughter—'Ha-ha-ha-ha-ha-ha!' (HE 245). The vocalic content can be varied to show the loud guffaw of the rustic, 'Haw-haw-haw!' (RN 262); the lighter laugh of a woman, 'Heu-heu-heu!' (RN 33); or a subtly graded set of sounds reproducing the tones of different characters in common mirth:

> 'Ho-ho-ho!' laughed dark Car.
> 'Hee-hee-hee!' laughed the tippling bride, as she steadied herself on the arm of her fond husband.
> 'Heu-heu-heu!' laughed dark Car's mother. (TD 84)

Other conventional signals can be similarly varied to suggest their intensity or purpose. The regular *sh* representing the sharply expelled breath which demands silence can be strengthened to 'ssh' (TD 15; JO 68) or to 'hsh' (JO 165). Prolongation of letters gives intensity to the exclamation of disgust, 'u-u-ugh!' (TM 227). Sometimes Hardy's invention moves from the more familiar graphological forms of representation and shows ingenuity in developing the common phonic associations of letters into new shapes. The hiss of contempt appears as 'Ts-s-s!' (MC 83) and as 'Piph-ph-ph!' (UG 113); a form of the latter serves also for a sigh of physical exhaustion as a bellringer finishes his ring—'Piph-h-h-h! A good forty minutes' (DR 447). The familiar 'tut, tut' is recognizable but given the impact of novelty as 'Tcht, tcht!' (DR 248). An old man's 'click' or implosive sound of self-congratulation is 'clk' (TM 212) or 'klk' (RN 163). The distortion which results from calling loudly to someone at a distance issues as 'Ho-i-i-i-i!' (UG 4) or as 'Hoi-i-i-i!' followed by 'Halloo-o-o-o!' (RN 33). The dairyman's call to his cows is visually strange and haunting in addition to its suggestion of a melancholy diphthong—'Waow! waow! waow!' (TD 136, 228). Effective as these graphologically realized signals are, one of Hardy's most evocative paralinguistic suggestions relies not on imitation but on simile—'Lord Mountclere sighed like a poet over a ledger' (HE 343).

The evidence of the novels shows Hardy as a writer notably sensitive to the human voice in its infinite variety. His attempts to bridge the gap between sounds heard and words read give him a high place among the novelists who have known that good fictional dialogue must be more than a transcription of words supposed to have been spoken. His achievement in the use of dialect sets him above most of his fellows, handling the unfamiliar variations with regard to character and situation and without distraction from the steady flow of the narrative. The criticism of contemporaries directed to the idiom of his peasant characters seems to have turned attention away from the problem which he himself pointed out: how to present living speech through a graphological system that lacks consistent phonetic correspondence with the spoken language. To adopt a metaphor which might have appealed to him, he orchestrated the speech of his many characters into the score of a rich and complex symphony.

# V

# Graham Greene at the Heart of the Matter

## ROGER SHARROCK

To talk of a change of direction in a writer's work is always to oversimplify; literary history tends to pin a personality within a too neat arrangement. In Greene's case the obsessional, neurotic drive constantly reasserts itself, so that it is nearer to the truth to express change as a reshuffling of the cards, not the introduction of a new pack. So if we take the card of the holy sinner, *The Heart of the Matter* belongs with his two preceding novels, *Brighton Rock* and *The Power and the Glory*. First, the depraved criminal who at least experiences the passage of holiness, then the ordinary sinner whom God and circumstances (which means God through his circumstances) compel into a saint: now an exceptionally good and honest man whom God's circumstances and his own needs compel into sin and crime and leave a question mark over his final end which is perhaps only suspended there for those unbelievers who persist in reading Catholic novels. The police chase which is an analogue of the divine hunting has now gone; but in its place is a police drama where the trap is slowly shutting, and not so much a divine hunt as a human escape from the responsibilities imposed by the divine.

Then if we take the card of place, Sierra Leone on the West African coast may, after Mexico, hardly seem to be a reshuffling at all. There is no temperate zone and moral issues steam and peel in the heat; if there is a distinction it is that the Mexico of *The Power and the Glory* was an indigenous suffering and dereliction, while Africa is a place for expatriates to lose their roots and go to pieces. Their books have to be wiped daily against the damp and discussions of modern poetry seem painfully trivial and irrelevant. Even voices change: 'Here intonations changed in the course of a few months: became high-pitched and insincere, or flat and guarded.' The country changes them and separates them from one another; in the first scene between Scobie and his wife she is separated from him by the mosquito netting under which she lies sick, with matted hair and closed eyes, resembling a dog or a cat in her complete prostration. Heat and sweat are everywhere a barrier: in bed Scobie tries to keep his body away from Louise: 'wherever they touched—even if it were only a finger lying against a finger—sweat started.'

Above all else the Coast tires its white people. The picture of a native porter bowing under his load dominates the imagery of the story. The image comes to be directed to Scobie, the chief character, who lives by shouldering other people's burdens:

> He was surprised how quickly she went to sleep: she was like a tired carrier who had slipped his load. She was asleep before he had finished his sentence, clutching one of his fingers like a child, breathing as easily. The load lay beside him now and he prepared to lift it.

The metaphor hovers over the whole story which may be read as an account of the increasing loads thrust upon Scobie until in his mere humanity he can no longer bear them. What he lacks and what he most desires is peace. His sense of the word is so profound that he is angry when his wife says he would have peace if she went away to South Africa:

> For he dreamed of peace by day and night. Once in sleep it had appeared to him as the great glowing shoulder of the moon heaving across his window like an iceberg, Arctic and destructive in the moment before the world was struck: by day he tried to win a few moments of its company, crouched under the rusting handcuffs in the locked office, reading the reports from the sub-stations. Peace seemed to him the most beautiful word in the language: My peace I give you, my peace I leave with you: O Lamb of God, who takest away the sins of the world, grant us thy peace. In the Mass he pressed his fingers against his eyes to keep the tears of longing in.

The wish for release of the conscientious administrator and husband is carried on to a different level by the language of the Mass; the peace offered by Christ is a positive, however unimaginable, not a mere release from human cares; we are reminded of the heaven of the sermon in *The Power and the Glory* which was something more than the absence of pain though the priest did not have the time to say what the something more might be. The search for an unattainable peace provides a counterpoint to the unrest in the foreground of the novel: Scobie finds it only in death when in his own mind he has inexorably cut himself off from Christ.

Scobie comes nearest to finding peace when he goes into the bush with his servant Ali to investigate the suicide of a District Commissioner. For this episode Greene draws on his first experience of West Africa, the arduous journey he made through Liberia with his cousin Barbara in 1935 described in the travel book *Journey Without Maps* (1936). Apart from this episode the setting of the novel and the white colony in Freetown are drawn from his experience in Sierra Leone in the war years as an intelligence agent (1941–3). On his journey up country Scobie dreams peacefully as he never does at home in Freetown:

> . . . a dream of perfect happiness and freedom. He was walking through a wide, cool meadow with Ali at his heels: there was nobody else anywhere in his dream, and Ali never spoke. Birds went by far overhead, and once when he sat down the grass was parted by a small green snake which passed on to his hand and up his arm without fear, and before it slid down into the grass again touched his cheek with a cold, friendly, remote tongue.

In the travel book Greene describes

> . . . the moments of extraordinary happiness, the sense that one was nearer than one had ever been to the racial source, to satisfying the desire for an instinctive way of life, the sense of release, as when in the course of psycho-analysis one uncovers by one's effort a root, a primal memory, should have been counterbalanced by the boredom of childhood too, that agonizing boredom of 'apartness' which came before one had learnt the fatal trick of transferring emotion, of flashing back enchantingly all day long one's own image, a period when other people were as distinct from oneself as this Liberian forest. I sometimes wonder whether, if one had stayed longer, if one had not been driven out again by tiredness and fear, one might have relearned the way to live without transference, with a lost objectivity.

The sense of peace and release from care is here compared to the repossession of the primary self achieved in psycho-analysis (no doubt with a side-glance at Greene's analysis under Richmond) and this in turn is equated with the state of childhood when people are seen as wholly other so that the painful and misleading transference of one's emotions to others which characterizes maturity is avoided. Scobie transfers his own emotion of devouring pity to others; he suffers in his person their immense need as he imagines it and in so

doing fails to grasp the facts of the case. The novel is problematic
unlike either of its predecessors: there is nothing problematic about
Pinkie's corruption—only over his final end does a question mark
stand; the indications of the whisky priest's sanctity are there though
muted—he is doubted only by himself and by the Pharisees, like the
woman in the prison cell; but Scobie has a question mark not only
over his spiritual destiny but also over his character as a man. Critics
have judged him to be a moral failure, an inferior person, or a
self-destructive neurotic: Or he has been described as 'a good man,
who loves too well but not wisely', a fairer and less captious reading
of the story. The possibility of different points of view on the
character shows how far Greene has entered on a new type of fiction.
While occupying opposite ends of the moral spectrum, Pinkie and
the whisky priest are united as representative figures, bearing the
cross of humanity under stress, endowed with a sense of the terror of
life and the possibility of damnation. Scobie is a man in a realistic
fiction with particular problems; whatever post-structuralists may
say of the writer's manipulation of the point of view in the classic
realist text, this has never prevented certain readers from finding
Fanny Price unbearable or entertaining a sneaking sympathy for
Becky Sharp. So the conduct of Scobie may remain open to different
interpretations, and to an even greater degree than in classical
realism, since as a twentieth-century man he has a problematic
relationship to his social environment. Life for the English officials in
West Africa is seen under the metaphor of a sickness: 'For fifteen
years he had watched the arrival of a succession of patients: peri-
odically at the end of eighteen months certain patients were sent
home, yellow and nervy, and others took their place.' The metaphor
of sickness continues though the climate that provides it may
change: it alters to the dangers of death and betrayal in wartime
London, and then back to Africa and the Congo in *A Burnt-Out Case*
with a real sickness, leprosy, as a metaphor for the progressive
degeneration of life. It is therefore apparent that however much
Scobie is presented as a man with particular problems and a certain
bent the novel yet retains a representative character on account of
Greene's habitual insistence, through imagery and authorial reflec-
tion, on the universality of his setting. The inference is, as the trap
Scobie has partly prepared for himself closes upon him, that elsewhere other traps are preparing, constructed of different materials.
The critics who condemn his moral and psychological weakness fail
to see that, as character is fate, so other characters may have other

fates. To allude to Hardy's quotation from Novalis reminds us that, like *The Mayor of Casterbridge* among Hardy's other work, *The Heart of the Matter* is the most purely an Aristotelian tragedy when set alongside Greene's other novels. Scobie's nobility is balanced on a fatal flaw and to dismiss him as an inferior human being is to allow oneself to forget within the academic pressure chamber that outside it both inferior and superior minds may succumb utterly to circumstances.

The environment that closes in so as to drive men to the breaking-point and their search for a peace that is denied are not the only themes that are repeated with variations from earlier books and are to occur again. Scobie is an interesting variation on the type of the just and weary policeman, the Assistant Commissioner of *It's A Battlefield*, for whom the prototype is Conrad's Commissioner in *The Secret Agent*. Scobie has the same asceticism, the same fear of retirement as these characters, and his chief calls him 'Scobie the Just'; but in the variation his fatal flaw of pity manoeuvres him into the position where he can be corrupted. The theme of the significant pathos of children or the innocent is also developed with variation. We have seen it first in *The Power and the Glory* in the precocious intelligence of Coral who has to die, in the priest's child who is lost, and in the dead Indian boy, an innocent victim. Children seem to be chosen as strikingly illustrating the utter proneness of human beings and the disparity between merit and reward. In *The Heart of the Matter* Scobie and his wife have a dead child Catherine who died in England before his wife came out to join him. Then there is the child who dies in the hospital at Pende after forty days' exposure in an open boat; Scobie is at the bedside and it is the most moving episode in the book. The most dreadful of questions for the Christian, the infliction of physical evil on the innocent of the world, is here fully engaged. It has been a crux of European ethics since the Lisbon earthquake in the eighteenth century, but in the twentieth century it has acquired a peculiar importance in liberal Western society: the declining belief in an after-life leaves nothing to compensate for the ills of this one, and tender sentiments towards the weak and helpless seem to have been developed in order to some extent to offset the appalling cruelties of the age towards many of the fit (so improved provision for the handicapped goes hand in hand with failure to suppress terrorism). In another novel, humanist not Catholic, but equally important as a moral barometer, Camus's *La peste*, the death of a young child in agony from bubonic plague brings together

Rieux the sceptic and the priest Paneloux in their common inability to understand why this should happen. Nineteenth-century writers were more inclined to treat the frequent early deaths of Paul Dombey and his contemporaries as a blessed return to an eternal home from which they had come trailing their clouds of glory. But if Greene shares with Camus a twentieth-century concern he also introduces a personal strain into the theme of the innocent child unnecessarily made to suffer. Scobie clearly identifies the six-year old girl at Pende with his daughter who died at that age. He prays, 'Father, give her peace. Take away my peace for ever, but give her peace.' His whole dedication to serving the right is concentrated in this single act of will; by the same act he surrenders the hope of peace only release from duty could give. Helen Rolt whom he is to love has survived the same open boat and at Scobie's first glimpse of her she is starved and immature-looking and clutching a child's stamp-album; she enters his life at the salient moment of the death of the child, and his love and pity are transferred from daughter to strange child to her: she is the first of a number of child-women who are appealing in their immaturity and who involve those who love them in disasters of which they are not the direct cause. Finally, while we consider the theme of the pathos of children, Ali, Scobie's 'boy', though a grown man, is a child in his trust and innocence, and his death is deliberately associated by Scobie with the death of his daughter Catherine and the expiation he feels he must make for that death and for all the other suffering for which he assumes responsibility. This act of expiation for Catherine, Ali, and the others leads up to the climax of the novel, and, in accordance with Greene's customary moral paradox, Scobie's act of atonement is one and the same with the supreme act of despair—suicide.

The complex and closely knit plot makes it difficult to separate any summary of the action from our grasp in detail of the characters and their inter-involvement. Scobie no longer loves his wife Louise who has become neurotic and irritable after the death of the child, but he feels pity and responsibility for her; a further blow to Louise is that he has been passed over for promotion. The driving impetus of the plot is his need to obtain sufficient money to enable her to go to South Africa for a time where he thinks she will be happier. It is wartime; there is much diamond smuggling from the interior to neutral ships passing through the port. A new commercial clerk, Wilson, is really an undercover intelligence agent sent to investigate the smuggling. He becomes romantically infatuated with

Louise who finds him a diversion from boredom since they can discuss poetry together; meanwhile Wilson is watching Scobie. Scobie accompanies the field-security police to search a Portuguese ship in the harbour, the *Esperança*; he finds a letter from the captain to his married daughter in Germany hidden in the lavatory cistern. The contents of the letter are innocuous and Scobie destroys it, feeling an obscure sympathy for the fat, sentimental captain who would lose his right of entry to the port if his offence against regulations is discovered. This episode is made to seem important because though Scobie's departure from duty may seem a minor one it is the beginning of a descent down a long slide and this is how he sees it:

> The scrap went up in flame, and in the heat of the fire another scrap uncurled the name of Groener. Fraser said cheerfully, 'Burning the evidence?' and looked down into the tin. The name had blackened: there was nothing there surely that Fraser could see—except a brown triangle of envelope that seemed to Scobie obviously foreign . . . Only his own heart-beats told him he was guilty—that he had joined the ranks of the corrupt police-officers.

Remaining righteous, he is not corrupted by money: he is corrupted by sentiment. The next step is when he is refused a loan by his bank manager and has recourse to the dubiously honest Syrian trader Yusef whom he suspects of dealing in contraband diamonds. He has in the past always refused the gifts Yusef has pressed upon him, and this is a perfectly proper arrangement on the surface, tied only to four per cent interest, but again his moral status has altered; the descent continues. He goes on an expedition up country to inspect the pathetic belongings of Pemberton, the young District Commissioner who has committed suicide. At the beginning of his own moral decline the reader is thus given a premonition of the final disaster in the death of an undeveloped boy who has left a pathetically schoolboyish letter of apology addressed to his father. Pemberton had been in debt to a shopkeeper who was an employee of Yusef: here and elsewhere the threads of the plot are kept extremely taut. As Scobie discusses the suicide letter with the local Catholic priest, Father Clay, the question of divine forgiveness is already raised, as it is again after Scobie's suicide at the end of the novel:

> He handed the letter to Father Clay. 'You are not going to tell me there's anything unforgivable there, Father. If you or I did it, it would be despair—I grant you anything with us. We'd be damned

all right because we know, but *he* doesn't know a thing.' 'The Church's teaching . . .' 'Even the Church can't teach me that God doesn't pity the young . . .'

It is because Pemberton had been young, unformed, that Scobie would forgive him and believes that God would forgive him; in a similar way he makes a concession for the Portuguese captain because he loves his daughter: 'That had been the turning point, the daughter.' Pemberton and the unknown daughter are shadows cast before; the ultimate and disastrous recipient of his pity is to be a young woman unformed in character like the one, and appearing to him as a substitute for his lost daughter.

The novel is divided into three books which present as in a tragedy the inevitable stages of a rounded action. At the end of the first, Scobie, having obtained the money, is able to see his wife off on the boat to South Africa. At the beginning of Book II he goes to Pende to receive the survivors from the torpedoed ship. He sits in the hospital by the bedside of the dying child and comforts her last moments by making the shadow of a rabbit's head on the wall with his hands. He meets Helen Rolt who has lost her husband in the open boat; he helps her, they become friends, and then lovers. After a quarrel caused by his limited, secret visits, he slips a letter confessing his love under the door of her hut. It is taken by Yusef's servant. He is now in Yusef's power and the inevitable blackmail follows: he is asked to take a packet of diamonds aboard the same Portuguese ship. This act closes with the unexpected return of Louise with the vague explanation that she is no longer worried about his being passed over for the Commissionership and that she must be there to keep him up to his religious duties.

The drama now moves inevitably to its close. Louise wants him to go to communion with her; in the confessional the priest, Father Rank, will not give him absolution since he will not promise to give up his adultery. He must at all costs keep up appearances as lover and husband to serve, in his view, the happiness of both women, and he goes to the altar with a clear-sighted expectancy of his own damnation. His betrayal of God coincides with the final stage of his corruption as a policeman. Before delivering the diamonds he has come needlessly to distrust his loyal servant Ali; Yusef promises in ambiguous terms to draw Ali away and in fact has him murdered. In an atmosphere of nightmare threat, drinking whisky with Yusef, it is an open question whether Scobie dimly understands the full impli-

cation of Yusef's reassurance, 'You will not have to worry, I will see
to that.' What is sure is that when he finds the body under some
petrol drums near the quayside he believes he is totally responsible
on account of his lack of trust, a deficiency in the virtue on which his
whole way of life is based, and that his betrayal is intimately connected with his betrayal of God. He sees Ali's body as 'like a broken
piece of the rosary . . . a couple of black beads and the image of God
coiled at the end of it'. Convinced that he has failed to give happiness
to either of the two women with whom he is involved, as well as in
his career, he carefully plans a suicide that will look like natural
death, for the sake of Louise's reputation and the insurance. He feigns
the symptoms of angina and obtains from his doctor the drug Evipan
(he has picked up a hint for this method from a woman doctor at a
dinner party); he then writes faked entries in his diary about his pains
and the regular doses he is taking, reserving enough tablets for a
massive overdose. Ironically, while he is putting his plan into action
he learns that the Commissioner-to-be has been posted to Palestine
and he will therefore be offered the coveted job after all. If he had
known this at the start there would have been no need specially to
comfort Louise, no need to place himself in Yusef's hands, no
opportunity to sleep with Helen: the closeness of the dramatic construction is nowhere more apparent than at this point. But Scobie
goes through with the suicide. The enigma of the last few minutes of
his life is passed on to the reader; as in the last night of the priest in
*The Power and the Glory* clues are offered which reflect back on the
course of his behaviour as well as pointing forward to his spiritual
future.

This is not the end. The end comes with the repercussions of his
death on the two women. Louise and Wilson talk about Scobie as
they examine his diary; they will probably marry, but not yet.
Wilson's training enables him to detect that some of the entries have
been made later in a different ink; and he knows that Scobie has been
receiving money from Yusef. We now learn that Louise came back
because she had been informed by a neighbour of the affair with
Helen; she can only tell Wilson that she thought he squared it with
his conscience by 'going to confession and starting over again'. This
reveals a complete misunderstanding of that moral scrupulosity, or,
if one likes, urge towards self-destruction, which prompts Scobie to
damn himself in preference to lying or to abandoning either of the
women to whom he feels obligation. Louise's only concern is that he
may, as Wilson guesses, have committed the unpardonable sin of

suicide: 'In spite of everything, he *was* a Catholic.' When she takes her suspicion to Father Rank he sums up in the manner of the old priest who confesses Rose at the end of *Brighton Rock*: 'The Church knows all the rules. But it doesn't know what goes on in a single human heart.' He adds that he thinks Scobie really loved God and when Louise breaks out bitterly, 'He certainly loved no one else', he replies that she may after all be right. The last we see of Helen is when she has come back slightly drunk from the beach with the crass Air Force officer, Bagster, who makes a crude attempt to seduce her. Her total apathy dissuades him and on his departure she is left vaguely thinking about God and trying to pray:

> . . . the wish struggled in her body like a child: her lips moved, but all she could think of to say was, 'For ever and ever, Amen . . .' The rest she had forgotten. She put her hand out beside her and touched the other pillow, as though perhaps after all there was one chance in a thousand that she was not alone, and if she were not alone now she would never be again.

As with the whisky priest's arousal of generosity in the dying American gangster, the effect of Scobie on other people is a testimony to his spiritual rightness. Helen had scoffed at his scruples about the sacraments, but she now enjoys an intimation of the presence of God, and it is as if his disinterested love has achieved the caring for her he desperately desired in his lifetime. This brief episode immediately precedes the interview between Louise and Father Rank. It is just as important in its way and carries more conviction: Father Rank's words have the finality of a pronouncement, even within the open, situational terms of Greene's moral theology, and therefore have, certainly for many non-Catholic readers, too much the air of imposed interpretation: the straight account of Helen's state of mind, from barren isolation to recognition of a reassuring otherness, is the best insight into what has gone on in Scobie's 'single human heart' and its living effect.

To put it crudely, Greene's Catholic novels, operating on the dangerous edge of things, begin by getting away with murder, then inebriety, then suicide. But we must look at the whole course of Scobie's behaviour, not just his taking his own life. There are two major difficulties, occurring respectively at the moral and religious levels of the novel; a separate examination of these difficulties may help us to reach beyond such an artificial separation of categories.

First, it is not easy to understand what constitutes the danger of pity, a danger that is continually stressed both in authorial comment and within Scobie's stream of consciousness. To be sure, we are shown, in the fashion of drama, how precise actions in the Yusef plot and in the Louise-Helen plot, produce a chain of events leading to a tragic outcome. But they might have done so had the spring of action been unscrupulous ambition in one case and romantic lust in the other. What is the nature of this pity that destroys—'this automatic terrible pity that goes out to any human need—and makes it worse' as Scobie says to himself when he begins to think that the emotion over-rides in him any real love for either woman? There is a perverse and idiosyncratic side to the presentation of how pity works: in regard to women it is excited by ugliness and failure, never by attractiveness:

> The greying hair, the line of nerves upon the face, the thickening body held him as her beauty never had. She hadn't put on her mosquito-boots, and her slippers were badly in need of mending. It isn't beauty that we love, he thought, it's failure—the failure to stay young for ever, the failure of nerves, the failure of the body. Beauty is like success: we can't love it for long.

If this pity has a perverse element about it, it always exonerates itself by dismissing its own cruelty in the very act of making a cruel judgement: 'His wife was sitting up under the mosquito-net, and for a moment he had the impression of a joint under a meat-cover. But pity trod on the heels of the cruel image and he hustled it away.' But how extraordinary to retreat like this from the pitilessness of style to the prepared pitifulness of response. The most dangerous heart of the book, its heart of the matter, lies in its projecting on to Scobie, the honest policeman, a painful sense of separation from other people which is disguised by the steadily maintained act of service. The guilt produced works both ways: Scobie can treat the subjects of his love as inferiors, and yet feel after all his day-to-day support for them 'the enormous breach pity had blasted through his integrity'. When he and Helen come together as lovers for the first time there is this same sense, from the prime actor's point of view, of an enemy lying in wait at the gates of love: 'What they had both thought was safety proved to have been the camouflage of an enemy who works in terms of friendship, trust and pity.' The enemy here is much more than passionate love which serves merely as a vehicle: the suggestion in both passages is that it is commitment to other persons which is ultimately destructive of the isolated self and its integrity. It may seem a paradox in Greene as a Christian writer that the supreme virtue of the Christian West, Shakespeare's 'naked new-born babe', should be viewed as dangerous. The paradox may be restated as an instance of the abrupt division between true Christianity and conventional codes of right and wrong which we have already met: a Christian morality involves sacrifice and this means the abandonment of the coded compromises by which the lonely self tries to exist in society.

The danger of the commitment to others brought by pity lies in our ignorance of other selves and therefore of their true needs. Scobie's bleak knowledge of the limits of human understanding makes him an unusually intellectual policeman—it should really be he, not Louise, who reads modern poetry; this aspect of his character comes perilously near to inhibiting the decisive actions he undertakes:

> If I could just arrange for her happiness first, he thought, and in the confusing night he forgot for the while what experience had taught him—that no one human being can really understand another, and no one can arrange another's happiness.

As he says to Louise of Pemberton's suicide, 'We'd forgive most things if we knew the facts.' But man never knows all the facts: Scobie's loyalty to the promises exacted by pity, to cherish Louise, to comfort Helen, bring despair into his heart long before the final realization of despair in suicide.

> Despair is the price one pays for setting oneself an impossible aim. It is, one is told, the unforgivable sin, but it is a sin the corrupt or evil man never practises. He always has hope. He never reaches the freezing-point of knowing absolute failure. Only the man of good will carries always in his heart this capacity for damnation.

So Scobie's plans are doomed from the outset since pity is blind to consequences and cannot see into the inner life of those whom it loves. It is a bitter joke that while he is at such pains to keep his affair with Helen secret his wife should know about it and take it in her stride, rejoining him from South Africa and hurrying him off to Mass with her, thus engineering his blasphemous communion and setting in train his suicide plan. Pity has more luck with children, and perhaps with Helen who is treated like a child. In children there is only a slender barrier between the inner and outer lives and therefore less room for inaccurate analysis. To use Greene's words in *Journey Without Maps*, they are distinct beings and do not flash back one's own image. Scobie's most vital and clearly judged act of pity is also his most disastrous: it is his prayer that his peace may be taken for ever if the dying six-year-old child may have peace. The implication is that his prayer is granted; the child is feverish and takes him for her father who died in the open boat; he eases her death by playing the rabbit game in her last moments; he certainly loses his peace for he has just met Helen Rolt, clutching her child's stamp-album, and the Yusef plot is closing in. To lose one's peace for ever is to be in hell and according to the law of the Church he has chosen hell when he takes communion in mortal sin and then again when he ends his own life. But an act of gratuitous sacrifice for a human being with whom he has no special ties (except the echo of his relationship to Catherine) is a purely Christian act. Furthermore his selflessness is persistent, not a sudden emotional volition: he had come to the hospital to be of use and had wanted least of anything to be left with a dying child; similarly, his care for Louise is expressed not by a single gesture of sacrifice (the loan from Yusef for the passage money) but by a steady effort in small things like prevailing upon her to nibble at her lunch. It now becomes apparent that what from the prudential human side is dangerous blind pity is from the religious side charity, a selfless and spontaneous love which resides in Christ and has therefore no need to calculate consequences.

If pity is really charity it is a character flaw only in human, prudential terms, and the moral and religious levels of the story are one and the same. But there yet remains a problem for many readers, Catholic and non-Catholic, in Scobie's ability to combine Christian charity with offences against moral and religious law, his adultery and his bad communion. The criticism usually is, not that he is a moral monster, but that he is an incredible character. The difficulty is best put, with the incisive commonsense we expect, by George Orwell:

> If he were capable of getting into the kind of mess that is des-
> cribed, he would have got into it earlier. If he really felt that
> adultery is mortal sin, he would stop committing it; if he persisted
> in it, his sense of sin would weaken. If he believed in Hell, he

would not risk going there merely to spare the feelings of a couple of neurotic women.

Orwell's points sound impressive but none of them stand up. They make Scobie seem an impossible character by ignoring the features which he shares with a tragic hero. The charge that he would have got into a mess earlier ignores the nature of tragedy, and the novel, which is to be about extraordinary, or at least outstanding events, and to begin at a certain point in time. Orwell's commonsense is betrayed by his agnosticism when he falls into the inaccuracy that adultery is only committed by enlightened liberals; and Scobie precisely does not persist in his adultery. The last point is a shrewd one, but it fails to take account of the impossible position into which he has manoeuvred himself, any more than it recognizes the charity which drives Scobie into accepting risks, in regard to his wife, and then on behalf of the dying child, long before he resigns himself to damnation. Orwell's reading, though perverse, does at any rate bring before us the full strain of the paradox by which virtuous intention commits sin and sin demonstrates saving love.

In fact Scobie is a man of good will who sins; it is not that he is unbelievable that upsets us: it is the extent of his goodness and of his sin that we, like Louise and Wilson, find alarming: he is indeed a moral monster, but then in Greene's view Christian morality, losing life to save it, is a monstrous form of behaviour. The intimations which link Scobie's actions with the sacrifice of Christ do this in an obscure way so that at some times he seems to be sharing the lot of the victim, at others to be inflicting pain on Christ or joining in his betrayal. This serves more than anything to sharpen the paradox of the virtuous sinner. When he has returned to his own house after the first night spent in Helen's quarters he reflects on the impossibility of his dual responsibility and the falsehood that will ensue: it is the interpretation of his action as treachery to God that is uppermost now:

> He had sworn to preserve Louise's happiness and now he had accepted another and contradictory responsibility. He felt tired by all the lies he would some time have to tell: he felt the wounds of those victims who had not yet bled. Lying back on the pillow he stared sleeplessly out towards the grey early morning tide. Somewhere on the face of those obscure waters moved the sense of yet another wrong and another victim, not Louise, not Helen. Away in the town the cocks began to crow for the false dawn.

Yet the echo of the cock crowing for Peter's betrayal is not allowed entirely to dominate the paragraph which forms the conclusion of the first part of the second book. The other wrong and the other victim move 'on the face of those obscure waters', and the Biblical allusion here adds to the crucified God the creative spirit of the first chapter of Genesis moving on the face of the waters. If Scobie's act is likely to inflict fresh pain on God it is also a part of God's creative plan; the confused images of creation and sacrifice suggest a fictional resolution of the perpetual problem of reconciling freewill with divine predestination.

At another time Scobie's desperate course seems to him the right one and the terms of ordinary morality are deliberately and para-doxically reversed. He thinks, as he walks towards her hut, that he will not go to Helen, his mistress, he could write to Louise and go to confession in the evening, and thus go to God: 'He would be at peace . . . Virtue, the good life, tempted him in the dark like a sin.' When he first begins to contemplate suicide he reflects that though the Church teaches it is the unforgivable sin, yet it is also taught that 'God had sometimes broken his own laws, and was it more impossible for him to put out a hand of forgiveness into the suicidal darkness and chaos than to have woken himself in the tomb, behind the stone?' Christ had not been murdered: you couldn't murder God: 'Christ had killed himself: he had hung himself on the Cross as surely as Pemberton from the picture rail.' To be sure, the strident tone of this passage reflects the distraught state of Scobie's mind and is not a statement of the author's theological opinion. However, when this obvious and necessary reservation is made, it still remains true that moral and theological judgements form the reflective consciousness of the whole novel and are not simply confined to Scobie's attitude; both the Portuguese captain and Yusef pronounce Scobie to be a good man, the latter on several occasions. It is particularly significant that the gross and slightly sinister Yusef who is always depicted shifting his weight in the chair from one thigh to the other should show a peculiar respect to Scobie; it is different from his superior officer's humorous regard for his professional probity: it is the unerring ability of wickedness to recognize the heart of goodness. But the theme of the virtuous sinner who may be saved at the last minute achieves its fullest exposition in the remarkable dialogue between Scobie and God which occurs after he has collected the package of Evipan:

I am going to damn myself, whatever that means. I've longed for peace and I'm never going to know peace again . . . No one can speak a monologue for long alone: another voice will always make itself heard: every monologue sooner or later becomes a discussion. So now he couldn't keep the other voice silent: it spoke from the cave of his body: it was as if the sacrament which had lodged there for his damnation gave tongue. You say you love me, and yet you'll do this to me—rob me of you for ever. I made you with love. I've wept your tears. I've saved you from more than you will ever know; I planted in you this longing for peace only so that one day I could satisfy your longing and watch your happiness. And now you push me away, you put me out of your reach. There are no capital letters to separate us when we talk together. I am not Thou but simply you, when you speak to me; I am humble as any other beggar. Can't you trust me as you'd trust a faithful dog? I have been faithful to you for two thousand years. All you have to do now is to ring a bell, go into a box, confess . . . the repentance is already there, straining at your heart. It's not repentance you lack, just a few simple actions: to go up to the Nissen hut and say good-bye. Or if you must, continue rejecting me but without lies any more. Go to your house and say good-bye to your wife and live with your mistress. If you live you will come back to me sooner or later . . .

The voice was silent in the cave and his own voice replied hopelessly: No. I don't trust you. I love you, but I've never trusted you. If you made me, you made this feeling of responsibility that I've always carried about like a sack of bricks . . . I can't shift my responsibility to you. If I could, I would be someone else. I can't make one of them suffer so as to save myself. I'm responsible and I'll see it through the only way I can. A sick man's death means to them only a short suffering—everybody has to die. We are all of us resigned to death: it's life we aren't resigned to.

So long as you live, the voice said, I have hope. There's no human hopelessness like the hopelessness of God. Can't you just go on as you are doing now? the voice pleaded, lowering the terms every time it spoke like a dealer in a market. It explained: there are worse acts. But no, he said, no. That's impossible. I love you and I won't go on insulting you at your own altar.

We are struck by the intense poignancy of simple language that somehow avoids sentimentality as it does at a different level in the episode of the dying child. But also remarkable is the attempt to dramatize God's totally loving relationship to his creation. Again the strange complementarity of divine purpose and individual freedom is touched upon; Scobie's sin would be arrogance in trying to arrange other people's lives as if he himself were God were it not for the revelation in this passage that he acts only in obedience to the impulses planted in him by his Creator. God lowers the price he asks and will presumably lower it still more; because he is a man of good will and wants only to safeguard others he may be saved from the impasse in which he has placed himself. But though the treatment of God's regard for the soul, his suffering on its behalf, and the intimate union the soul enjoys when it accepts the divine love, is theologically tactful and spiritually sensitive, the passage does not avoid the more subversive implications of the theme of the virtuous sinner. Thus the reference to the sacraments comes dangerously near to treating them as mechanical tokens of obedience rather than vehicles of grace ('the repentance is already there, straining at your heart'). And since if the clues are to be followed Scobie is apparently saved at the end, then the Catholic sacramental system, if it is not to be abandoned to the *faux dévots*, must be viewed as a sort of framework of reference *pour encourager les autres*. This would be an alarming conclusion, but less alarming than to conclude that Scobie is abandoned by God and not saved. A solution to the difficulty is to be found if we follow the hints of the story and perceive that total responsibility assumes total risk in treading the tightrope of Christian moral action and that when Scobie takes the overdose he enters a sphere where rules are no longer applied, but where exceptions are made, as they have to be made for other erring individuals. All are individually lost, and all may be saved individually through no virtue of their own. This is suggested by the lines of Rilke Scobie reads in Louise's book when he has said goodnight to her for the last time:

> We are all falling. This hand's falling too—
> all have this falling sickness none withstands.
>
> And yet there's always One whose gentle hands
> this universal falling can't fall through.

The lines sound to him like truth but he rejects them as sounding too comfortable; he cannot pray or trust and is as doubtful of his own future as the whisky priest: 'I slip between the fingers, I am greased with falsehood, treachery: trust was a dead language of which he had forgotten the grammar.' But when he has taken the drug and tried unsuccessfully to say an act of contrition while remaining on his feet, he has the same experience as Pinkie in his last hour of a presence from outside striving to enter in. 'It seemed to him as though someone outside the room were seeking him, calling him, and he made a last effort to indicate that he was here.' Someone is appealing for help, someone has need of him, and 'automatically at the call of need, at the cry of a victim, Scobie strung himself to act'. From the depths of his consciousness, and most characteristically, from the depth of his isolation, he responds to the cry of suffering as he had done with the human beings he could not understand, and brings himself with a great effort to say aloud, 'Dear God, I love . . .' When he falls to the floor the medal of the obscure Portuguese saint given him by the captain comes away. This last touch is no mere item of piety since whatever intercession is involved the medal takes us back to the moment in the cabin when the whole course of events began; then Scobie acted with disinterested generosity towards the captain who responded with the spontaneous gesture of a simple man: the medal stands for all that, and sums up the continual work of pity which Scobie brings to completion by pitying God himself in his unfinished prayer.

The older Greene has not handled Scobie as gently as I have done, and as many readers would wish him handled. Nor is his later opinion of the novel as a whole at all sympathetic. On his own work a writer is merely one more critic but Greene's afterthought on *The Heart of the Matter* is interesting not only because it runs counter to the present approach but because it is illustrative of a wholly different point of view from that implicit in the Catholic novels.

> The scales to me seem too heavily weighted, the plot overloaded, the religious scruples of Scobie too extreme. I had meant the story of Scobie to enlarge a theme which I had touched on in *The Ministry of Fear*, the disastrous effect on human beings of pity as distinct from compassion. I had written in *The Ministry of Fear*: 'Pity is cruel. Pity destroys. Love isn't safe when pity's prowling round.' The character of Scobie was intended to show that pity can be the expression of an almost monstrous pride.

In *The Ministry of Fear*, the most fantastic and the most personal of the entertainments, Arthur Rowe kills his wife to relieve her from agonizing pain. Yet later he suspects that it was his own pain in watching her, not hers, he was relieving. All his conduct is governed by 'that sense of pity which is so much more promiscuous than lust'. But the rhetoric here would brand the pity as a personal indulgence while admitting that it is, in a Christian and Kantian manner, extended to all regardless of personal interest. Whatever Greene says of the ghost in the machine we can only judge Rowe and Scobie by their actions and their actions are disinterested which is why they are sometimes disastrous. Greene is more persuasive when he speaks of technical faults in *The Heart of the Matter* which allow the reader to think of Scobie as a good man hounded by the harsh demands of his wife; we only see Louise through his eyes, and a concession in the narrative to her point of view (apparently present in the original draft) might have shown her in a more favourable light and Scobie in a less. Louise is undoubtedly a narrow character, narrow in her religious and aesthetic stock responses and in the scope given to her by the novelist. But the great drawback to accepting Greene's reading of his own novel is that there is only one character to express the emotion of compassion as distinct from pity and that is the God who hovers on the edge of the narrative in the dialogue with Scobie already quoted. Since Scobie's point of view is dominant we are obliged to believe that no loving understanding of other human beings is possible: everywhere a moral mosquito netting occludes our vision. However, if God can both love and understand, and thus turn pity into compassion, this surely is enough for the whole world of separated monads. It gives us a strange sort of novel, one in which God is felt not simply as an influence but as a character, though a partly hidden character, at the climax of the book. To employ Northrop Frye's nomenclature, Greene at this point departs from the customary limitations of the novel (ordinary men and women as characters, formal realism) and passes over into romance, the form he had practised in his first incursions into prose fiction and to which he has always been attracted: *The Ministry of Fear* is sprinkled with allusions to Charlotte M. Yonge's *The Little Duke*. The characters of romance tend to become psychological archetypes: the final step has been taken when the Form lying behind all archetypes is introduced, for then fiction must come to an end. Or to put it in another way, God cannot be a character in realistic fiction since he is the One and it is an imitation of the Many.

The presence of God, or at least of the voice of God, in this single episode breaks into the narrative realism of *The Heart of the Matter* and is more startling than it might have appeared against the black-and-white morality pattern of the two previous Catholic novels. For realism is of its nature the semblance of the real and cannot therefore admit divinity except as the intimation of presence, as in Pinkie's perception in *Brighton Rock* of something outside the car window. But Greene's criticism of the novel concentrates only on what he considers to be technical faults such as the partial treatment of Louise and the sketchy characterization of Wilson. He concludes:

> Maybe I am too harsh to the book, wearied as I have been by reiterated arguments in Catholic journals on Scobie's salvation or damnation. I was not so stupid as to believe that this could ever be an issue in a novel. Besides I have small belief in the doctrine of eternal punishment (it was Scobie's belief not mine). Suicide was Scobie's inevitable end; the particular motive of his suicide, to save even God from himself, was the final twist of the screw of his inordinate pride. Perhaps Scobie should have been a subject for a cruel comedy rather than for tragedy . . .

But Scobie's immediate response to an appeal for help is not on reading either ignoble or comic; one can understand the author's objection to criticism which has treated the book as a theological essay, but his account applies more to intention than execution. Scobie does not appear as inordinately proud in his behaviour to any of those he is associated with; salvation and damnation are issues kept in the forefront because Scobie, the dominant 'point of view', keeps them there after his desperate decision: Greene admits that Scobie is based on nothing but his own unconscious, and if he is a monster it is not through monstrous pride but on account of his absurd attempt at pure moral action in a fallen world: this involves the breaking of codes, the fall into sin, and ultimate pardon. Greene in his later novels, from *A Burnt-Out Case* onwards, has become a predominantly comic writer, as he states in the 1974 preface to that novel; so looking back he has little sympathy for his Christian tragedy. His remarks, framed in the terms of comic art, technique and moral comment, help to isolate the special quality of the five Catholic novels which subordinate the moral life to a religious standard based on the four last things, death, judgement, heaven and hell. The retrospective condemnation of theological criticism is primarily directed against the purely rational approach that would turn human behaviour, real or fictional, into precisely demarcated issues and solutions. The human heart moves in ways of which reason knows nothing; so does God. God comes to Scobie unexpectedly at the end, as He had come to the whisky priest. It is like his description of the death of his admired Rochester: 'If God appeared at the end, it was the sudden secret appearance of a thief, not a State entrance heralded by the trumpets . . .' So the later comic Greene, anxious to disclaim the role of theological propagandist imposed upon him by over-enthusiastic Catholic critics, has this at least in common with the author of the Catholic novels written between his thirty-third and forty-sixth years: he believes with Pascal that *le coeur a ses raisons que la raison ne connaît pas* and that God and man both move in mysterious ways.

Comedy was always waiting in the wings of the drama of extreme religious commitment or extreme denial. It is already there in the earlier novels, in Minty in *England Made Me* with his seedy and secret life, in the episode of the medical rag during a gas practice in *A Gun for Sale* which results in the deflation of the pathetically hearty Buddy Ferguson; it is refined in the treatment of the Lehrs in *Brighton Rock*; in *The Heart of the Matter* it flickers uncertainly, its critical spirit uneasy on the edge of the central absolutes. Wilson and Harris, the two new colonial officials, pass the time in cockroach-killing contests and plan to organize an Old Downhamians annual dinner at which they will be the only members of the school. Uncertainty is declared by the element of farce here. Wilson is a draft for a character, one whom Greene admits in retrospect obstinately refused to come alive when the novel was being written. Wilson's love for Louise is romantic and immature; he publishes in the *Old Downhamian* a poem in which he sees himself as Tristram in the legend. In a scene which has no organic relation to the story he goes to a native brothel and waits for a girl to be brought to him. The implication is that his mawkish idealism and half-guilty lust are two sides of the one coin; he is an undeveloped personality, and in spite of, or perhaps because of this scene, and his mastery of the techniques of secret intelligence, he carries throughout an air of spoiled innocence: Louise will be able to manage him as she could never manage Scobie. There hangs over him a statement about the failure of innocence and the undeveloped English public school heart which never quite gets made. Greene's critique of false innocence has its origins in the introspection of the hero in *The Man Within*; Anthony Farrant in *England Made Me* is a variation on the theme; it is developed most fully and successfully in the study of Pyle in *The Quiet American*. The belief in ideals having a reality quite apart from the facts of experience is always a target for Greene's serious comedy; it is the prime mark of false innocence, and is allied to the religious dogmatism which has no respect for life as it is lived which is also a constant target. This theme and other comic themes are handled more expansively in the novels of the next decade.

If Louise is too narrowly presented and Wilson is too inconclusive (an outline of a problem rather than a man), Yusef is powerfully conceived and realized and it is no wonder his creator was still pleased with him when he wrote the preface for the collected edition. The germ is a certain sinister villain of popular fiction who is a big man physically (a Sidney Greenstreet role in film thrillers of the period). Quite beyond the shiftiness of a man living on his wits he is endowed with a psychological depth and a remarkable sensitiveness which responds to Scobie's humanity even while he perceives his weakness. The combination of wiliness and sensitivity gives him more control over events than any other character; he can say with authority to Scobie: 'One day you will come back and want my friendship. And I shall welcome you.' Scobie sees in his blackmailer 'his only companionship, the only man he could trust'. His progressive surrender is indicated by the places they meet in, Yusef's car, his own house, Yusef's house, and finally Yusef's private office. The diction of an intelligent uneducated man to whom English is a second language is unerringly caught without attempt at pidgin or broken speech; it foreshadows the skill in rendering Wordsworth's speech in *Travels with My Aunt*:

> The Royal Ordnance Corps have very fine actors and they have made me appreciate the gems of English literature. I am crazy about Shakespeare. Sometimes because of Shakespeare I would like to be able to read, but I am too old to learn. And I think perhaps I would lose my memory. That would be bad for business, and though I do not live for business I must do business to live. There are so many subjects I would like to talk to you about. I should like to hear the philosophy of your life.

Yusef is drawn with remarkable verbal economy. There are few physical touches other than his hairy chest and his habit of shifting from one huge thigh to the other when sitting. He is less in front of the reader than Wilson, and does not function as a consciousness in the narrative, as Wilson does in the brothel scene and for a few minutes with Louise when his declaration of love is interrupted by a humiliating nose-bleed. Yusef rises above the indecisiveness of the other minor characters because he is Mephistophilis to Scobie's Faust, the cruel servant to one who is the constant servant of others.

In *The Heart of the Matter* the expressionist poetry of the earlier novels has been largely dried out. Similes are subdued, less frequent, and more functional: 'Thin black bodies weaved like daddy-long-legs in the dimmed highlights.' The focus on particular recurring images is likewise more purposeful, less surreal. The rusty handcuffs hanging on the wall behind Scobie's desk are the symbol of his job and also of his imprisonment by pity which finally immobilizes him. The stamp album clutched by Helen Rolt on the stretcher focuses on her childishness which excites his pity; it also works in terms of plot allowing him an excuse to continue his visits by bringing stamps to her. Wilson's ill-fitting tropical suit of peculiar hue speaks of something unsuitable and inwardly false in his nature. Together with the less obtrusive imagery a new vein of detached moral comment is opened which anticipates the authorial wisdom of the later comic novels; in this book, however, the comment is expressed, sometimes incongruously, through the consciousness of Scobie. Believing miserably in a moral solipsism which leaves pity as the only bridge to other human selves he reflects: 'Point me out the happy man and I will point you out either egotism, selfishness, evil—or else an absolute ignorance.' But it is the man of good will who is ignorant of what goes on in other minds and who wonders painfully whether, if only he knew the facts, he would have to feel pity even for the planets, 'if one reached what they called the heart of the matter'. In the novel that escaped Greene's intention it is only God who can effectively pity and succour the creation he has left so calamitously broken.

# VI

# Modernism and Englishness: Reflections on Auden and Larkin

## EDWARD NEILL

Like *non Angli sed Angeli*, the profoundly important distinction 'not modern—modernist' can easily acquire the status of a joke, and Bradbury and McFarlane rightly point up the awkwardness ('semantic instability'[1] is their phrase) of the term. The modern is, modernism was—certainly. But what was modernism? Hardly a set of rules or even, loosely, a 'regulative concept'—after all, 'examples' are rather more important than precepts here. On the other hand, as a 'historical phenomenon' it also refuses to 'reify'. Though not an entity, as P.N. Furbank wittily puts it, 'trying to break out, like dry rot, all over the place', he himself does make 'it' sound rather like that as he moves on to observe that 'culture in this period (c.1900) was peculiarly cosmopolitan: Paris was aware of Vienna, and Vienna of St Petersburg . . .'[2]

Highly retrospective quasi-historical designations like 'modernism' tend in any case to be movable feasts, at once more and less than the apparent sums of their parts, as 'the Renaissance', a comparable instance, is 'more than Leonardo da Vinci, the Medici, Shakespeare and Machiavelli' but less than just the historical period, *tout court*—whenever it was. 'Modernism', too, becomes vacuous, a 'sovereign ghost', if used as a chronological hold-all for what Furbank calls 'all the new thought that was developing round about 1900–10'. Gabriel Josipovici will give us a more generous helping of 1880–1920.[3] Peter Faulkner, in his modest, stimulating book on the subject gives it a provisional justification which comes near the present theme when he says that the term's utility is 'proved by the fact that an important modern writer like Orwell is not usually thought of as a modernist and that the relation of D.H. Lawrence to the idea is far from

---

[1] *Modernism 1890–1930*, ed. M. Bradbury and James McFarlane (Sussex, 1978), pp. 22–3.

[2] P.N. Furbank and Arnold Kettle, *Modernism and its Origins* (Milton Keynes, 1975), p. 5.

[3] Gabriel Josipovici, *The Lessons of Modernism and Other Essays* (London, 1977), p. 109.

simple'.[4] The word 'idea' here is perhaps a blemish, but the idea itself is a sound one.

It is interesting that the writers mentioned here as specifically problematic are often thought of as being quintessentially English, witting contributors to what Peter Ackroyd has called 'the myth of England'—'I am English, and my Englishness is my very vision;'[5] although of course one can and does willingly concede that varieties of Englishness are likely to prove as various as those of 'modernism' itself.

Curiously enough, in this last (non-posthumous) work of F.R. Leavis,[6] himself often thought of as the most sturdily indigenous, the most unmodishly uncosmopolitan of all our critics, Lawrence is prone to look even more 'modernist' than previously, particularly in the feeling one gets of his 'sailing into the unknown', improvising at the pitch of genius. This last phrase is also a quotation, this time from M.L. Rosenthal,[7] who uses it to convey his sense of modernist originality. Risk, to remember a late phrase by Robert Lowell, becomes the artist's *métier*. What implicitly dissolves in this exploration is any clear commitment to readerly expectations, unless, perhaps, those should happen to coincide with those of Joyce's 'ideal reader suffering from an ideal insomnia'. It is interesting to note that it was precisely on such grounds that Auden pronounced Joyce to be 'mad'.

Here, at any rate, Lawrence's baffled sense of moving about in worlds not realized when he writes to A.D. Macleod in April 1913 that he is 'doing a novel which [he] has never grasped' and 'can only just make out what it is about' sounds modernist, though hardly in the easy, emancipated vein of a Wallace Stevens observing scornfully no doubt, to Robert Frost, 'You write on subjects.' He meant, of course, 'You are not a modernist like me,' but, perhaps mercifully, hadn't the word for it, for the word only came into vogue when the *thing* had disappeared, and even Hugh Kenner, modernism's most provocative advocate, did not favour the term for his enormously ambitious synthesis of the bearings of modernism, *The Pound Era*

[4] Peter Faulkner, *Modernism* (London, 1977), p. ix.

[5] D.H. Lawrence in a letter of 21 October 1915 used as epigraph to Leavis's *D.H. Lawrence: Novelist* (London, 1955).

[6] F.R. Leavis, *Thought, Words and Creativity: Art and Thought in Lawrence* (London, 1976).

[7] M.L. Rosenthal, *Sailing into the Unknown: Yeats, Pound and Eliot* (New York, 1978).

(1971). It remains the most wide-ranging investigation of 'its' procedures, as well as the most committed, like his earlier book on Eliot,
*The Invisible Poet*, to attacking what he called an 'incredibly illiterate
literary generation' in England—then (c.1920).

P.N. Furbank, in England now, concedes the point. He depicts an
Edwardian England of some backwardness, for whom the 'disten-
sions of Empire', in Poundian phrase, entailed a measure of cultural
insulation, while Samuel Hynes claims that 'the new thought of
Europe had been kept out of England, as though by quarantine.'[8]

Contentious and even exasperating, such claims often appear
to presuppose that there is something called modernism which
is simply the repository of all artistic virtue, that modernism in
England must mean modernism with backspin or predictably result
in a simple-minded exhortation to play up, play up and play the
game of knowledge. A creative effort like that of Virginia Woolf,
where we can set the attacks on solid-puddingy crowd-pleasing
novelists like Bennett and Galsworthy against her profoundly un-
satisfactory response to *Ulysses*, is inherently a case of considerable
complexity. Attempts at a thoroughgoing 'annulment' of all that
'modernism' stood for only really appear a generation later, in
Kingsley Amis, for example, whose professional *persona*, as Blake
Morrison's book makes clear, included as it were *de rigueur* the philis-
tine hearty and the treasonable clerk.[9]

In Auden, however, we might reasonably say, 'the necessaries are
embarked'. His idea of poetry as a 'game' of knowledge sounds
'reassuring' in a disconcerting way, while his view of the poet
seemed to reify falsely as a particular kind of person, a person in some
respects not unlike the late Kenneth Tynan, with his liking for
spectacular events like bullfights and displays of pyrotechnics, a
person of immensely prolonged adolescence with conjugations of
the verbs *étonner* and *épater* stencilled on his brow, a person, that is,
corresponding to one side of Auden's own inherently 'double'
nature. Of course we have to remind ourselves that under the sway
of the anxiety of influence poets do characteristically work by means
of subversion and annulment, which is precisely their way of

---

[8] Samuel Hynes, *The Edwardian Turn of Mind* (Princeton, 1967), p. 308.
[9] Blake Morrison, *The Movement: English Poetry and Fiction of the 1950's*
(Oxford, 1980). See, e.g. p. 132: 'Here they come—tramp, tramp, tramp—all
those characters you thought were discredited or had never read or (if you
are like me) had never heard of—Barbusse, Sartre, Camus, Kierkegaard . . .'
(from a review of Colin Wilson's *The Outsider*).

'making it new', as modernism's most jaded tag has it.

Besides, he had, as it were, a stab at modernism. His early poems were without titles, only numbered, looking like poems looking for subjects, or poems whose subjects had to be divined or intuited by the reader. Again, the prankish early habit, described by Isherwood, of salvaging lines from poems to 'plug' later ones with looks like an unauthentic attempt to carry on modernist *collage*, while the principle of obscurity, sometimes made respectable as a principle of complexity, in Auden sometimes becomes a principle of obfuscation, for example in the unorthodoxly 'psychoanalytic' 'Sir, no man's enemy . . .', where 'will his negative inversion' and other phrases look wilful, though his own later objection to the end of the poem perhaps misunderstands it, as its unremitting 'not-quitenesses' can invest the injunction to 'look smiling at/ New styles of architecture' with sufficiently sardonic overtones to accommodate his personal dislike of 'new styles of architecture'. Here as elsewhere he seems insufficiently aware of his poetic capacity for polysemy or fruitful equivocation.

A notable instance of this capacity for ambiguity bafflingly deployed is 'Under Which Lyre', in which Apollo, god of bureaucrats, dutiful poetry and literal-mindedness (rather like the Apollo of a famous epigram by Hölderlin) is routed by Hermes. The poem seems to me to be a profoundly Apollonian utterance, nowhere more than in its closing lines, supposedly part of a 'Hermetic Decalogue', in which we are told to:

'Read the *New Yorker*, trust in God,
And take short views.'

It has been said that Auden's life (or biography) is irrelevant to his poems, but anyone who has immersed himself in Carpenter's work will see, for example, that his early 1940's New York *ménage*, a Bohemian household he 'ran' with 'nursery strictness', but which was condemned by the more 'Kensingtonian'[10] Benjamin Britten and Peter Pears as 'sordid beyond belief'[11], was a positive expression of his own personal contradictions, in which:

---

[10] Auden described Britten's *Midsummer Night's Dream* as 'pure Kensington'. See Humphrey Carpenter, *W.H. Auden: A Biography* (London, 1981), p. 428.

[11] Carpenter, p. 304. The actual phrase was Peter Pears's.

> Falstaff the fool confronts forever
> The prig Prince Hal.

Though an indefatigable Prince Hal to the raffish inmates of Middagh Street's 'bawdy house'[12], that was not enough to prevent his seeming a little too much of the Falstaff to the perhaps on this occasion faintly priggish Pears and Britten. Perhaps more and more he came to see his quasi-impersonal constatations as expressions of his own nature, and in old age he became simply personal. The strong-lined difficulty of the earlier poems already contrasts strongly with the slackened, coherent, near-*reportage* of a poem like 'Dover'. The frequent 'sort of Anglo-Saxon' lines in his early poems, alliterated, four-beat, and with a 'defamiliarizing' continence in the use of the definite and indefinite articles contrasts with a later rush of definites, perhaps because it helps reinforce an assumption of shared experience, as in T.S. Eliot's 'The vanished power of the usual reign' of *Ash Wednesday*, which was obviously such a strong influence.

Another well-known poem, 'Our Hunting Fathers', looks 'modernist' in its intricacy, its impersonality, and its hunger to transform history into myth. The notion that the love of 'rational' creatures should be creation's 'crowning glory' is undercut by the dismayed realization that love is suited to 'the intricate ways of guilt'. But all this masks the almost confessional last lines in which it is love's lot:

> To hunger, work illegally
> And be anonymous

—as 'illegally' refers fairly plainly to the (then) illegality of the homosexual act, especially if we think of 'anonymous' as referring to 'the love that dare not speak its name'. *A Reader's Guide to W.H. Auden* appears innocent of such considerations, either because they are too obvious or because the rather studied and mannered 'complexity' of the poem appears to make the main task of 'exegesis' lie elsewhere. In this respect the poem is itself an intricate way of guilt.

A poem which looks much more like a deliberate attempt to be what one might call the 'obverse' of modernism, of *The Waste Land*, for example, for whose 'hysterical sublime', as an Oxonian non-

---

[12] Carpenter, p. 304. This was a reporter's mishearing of 'boarding house'.

admirer[13] called it, he substitutes an unbuttoned, expansive, continuous, formally organized, discursive, chatty, comic, perhaps
slightly middle-brow antithesis, cued by Byron, the most outgoing,
unarty and bisexual of the Romantic poets, is the 'Letter to Lord
Byron'. In deliberate contrast to *The Waste Land*, commercial/
industrial 'landscapes' are found congenial:

> Tramlines and slagheaps, pieces of machinery,
> That was, and still is, my ideal scenery.

'Doubleness' recurs, however, because although he conspires with
the spirit of Byron to make fun of Wordsworth, his comments on the
blighting effects of industrialism make him brush past Wordsworth's own phrasing:

> There on the old historic battlefield
> The cold ferocity of human wills . . .

But where he contradicts himself most, again in a way that seems to
preclude self-knowledge, is in his impassioned address to (and
against) 'Normality', 'hailed' as a 'goddess of bossy underlings',
because the whole posture and style of the poem seem bent on
reasserting it/her. Ghoulishly intent on being seen as a kind of
poetical train emerging with a cheerful toot from the gloomy tunnel
of 'modernism', he hails the eighteenth century as a time when the
artist was dependent on his 'public' and 'had to please or go without
his food', which is not very nice if you happen to think of Mozart
going without his—a sign, perhaps, that his eye is on 'modernism',
not Mozart. Again, a line like:

> I bought and praised but did not read Aquinas

is hugely redolent of *relief* that the poet can be healthily candid,
apparently, and need no longer mime that terrifying 'Mind of
Europe' which 'abandons nothing *en route*', and which seems at times
to be a presence in T.S. Eliot's poems as well as his famous essay,
'Tradition and the Individual Talent'.

In this poem, too, a particular *bête noire* is Ezra Pound, whose
fractured polyglottal opacities make no sense in a poem of this sort,

---

[13] F.W. Bateson, *Essays in Critical Dissent* (London, 1972), p. 138.

light-versical as it is (though that 'light verse' is simply the 'opposite of modernism' as P.N. Furbank appears to believe, is partly denied by the modernists' own practices and partly by a poem like Auden's 'The Fall of Rome', which does what one critic saw as a key procedure of *The Waste Land* in 'manipulating a continuous parallel between antiquity and modernity'). Here, installed in his Icelandic quarters:

> *Ich hab' zu Haus, ein Gra, ein Grammophon.*
>  *Les gosses anglais aiment beaucoup les machines.*
>  *To καλον. Glubit. Che* . . . what this may mean
> I do not know, but rather like the sound
> Of foreign languages like Ezra Pound.[14]

Adding insult to injury, this contrives to suggest both that Pound specialized in the *sound* of foreign languages and that Pound is *himself* a foreign language. Also it refuses to imitate Pound's procedures and improve on them, which would be correct modernist procedure. It merely reduces them to rubble.

In yet another famous poem we can trace what appears to be a specific attempt to annul a key modernist injunction. In moving towards an insistence that 'the natural object is always the *adequate* symbol', Pound warns not to 'use an expression like "dim lands *of peace*". It dulls the image'.[15] The third song in a sequence of 'Ten Songs' seems to luxuriate in the flouting of this advice:

> Warm are the still and lucky miles,
> White shores of longing stretch away,
> A light of recognition fills
>    The whole great day, and bright
> The tiny world of lovers' arms.

Most of my examples so far, which could of course be endlessly elaborated and added to, have referred to Pound and Eliot. But this most specific instance of attempted 'disconfirmation' comes in his 'In Memory of W.B. Yeats', where he cries in Yeats's teeth, as it were, that 'poetry makes nothing happen'. This, again, is intended to

---

[14] This stanza is cut in his *Collected Poems*. See *The English Auden: Poems, Essays and Dramatic Writings, 1927–1939*, ed. Edward Mendelson (London, 1977), p. 169–70.
[15] *The Literary Essays of Ezra Pound* (ed. T.S. Eliot) (London, 1954), p. 5.

reduce to rubble what he would see as the hubris of Yeatsian 'conscience'. When Yeats writes, in 'The Man and the Echo':

> Did that play of mine send out
> Certain men the English shot?

Auden wants this to be seen as more self-flattering and self-deluding
than self-accusing. When, Auden continues, in a key phrase, which
he repeats, 'it [poetry] survives', he is certainly to my mind invoking
the French aristocrat who, asked what he had done in the French
Revolution, replied 'I survived'. This is brilliant, I feel, because he is
at once confirming the notion that art is 'aristocratic' and refusing to
confirm his 'corollary', that art is socially efficacious or momentous
in the way that Yeats thinks desirable (though, again, as John Bayley
shows in *The Romantic Survival*, Auden's own attitude to the social
function of art is as interestingly muddled as anyone else's). Unfortunately, here his elaboration of the idea is also unhappy, as he
goes on to call poetry 'a way of happening, a mouth', which seems to
call on the reader to think in terms of a way of happening that makes
nothing happen, a mouth that makes nothing happen.

Finally, a particularly head-on attempt to 'dispose' of the sus-
pected 'art-worship' of the modernists would appear to be the 'deep
abhorrence' voiced in 'Letter to Lord Byron':

> If I caught anyone preferring Art
> To Life and Love and being Pure-in-Heart.

In fact in context these lines are far from being unambiguous, but
they do seem to be written to please Nanny, and the semi-explicit
idiom of 'catching someone at it' seems schoolmasterish, and perhaps leaves one to boggle at what form the 'preferring' would
actually take.

However, these lines were held up for admiration as a kind of
English and anti-modernist touchstone by Philip Larkin in a review
of *Homage to Clio* in *The Spectator*. Indeed, though in Auden we often
have a sense of a naughty, even gleeful flouting of what he takes to be
modernist precept and example, Larkin's seems at first sight a much
more deliberate 'programme' of dismantling and demolition of
modernist assumptions and procedures. An obvious technical difference is that the modernist urge to be technically experimental if
not metamorphic is rejected. (He quotes with relish Wilde's observation that 'only mediocrities develop'.) 'To break the pentameter,

that was the first heave' is the most literal injunction of the kind.
Larkin, however, not only 'mends' the pentameter, he fills up his
pentametery lines with contemporary detail so that lines like:

Canals with floatings of industrial froth

from 'The Whitsun Weddings', or:

The jabbering set he egged her on to buy

from 'Mr Bleaney' proclaim as specifically as may be that they are
'modern, not modernist'. Again, where Pound will tell us to 'go in
fear of abstractions' Larkin will let them run riot, as he does in an
exceptionally interesting poem, 'Here', the first in *Whitsun Weddings*,
where abstractions—loneliness, silence, distance, existence—
positively take over:

> where removed lives
>
> Loneliness clarifies. Here silence stands
> Like heat. Here leaves unnoticed thicken,
> Hidden weeds flower, neglected waters quicken,
> Luminously-peopled air ascends:
> And past the poppies bluish neutral distance
> Ends the land suddenly beyond a beach
> Of shapes and shingle. Here is unfenced existence:
> Facing the sun, untalkative, out of reach.

It seems a logical development of this cluttered, portentous poem,
which seems to be much more experientially 'open' than many of the
others, which will readily X-ray to show thesis : antithesis :
annulment as something like their underlying, foreclosed structure.
It is a poem that is in such an unseemly hurry to depersonalize itself
that the first main verb, deferred until the second stanza, has no
'proper' subject:

> Swerving east, from rich industrial shadows
> And traffic all night north; swerving through fields
> Too thin and thistled to be called meadows,
> And now and then a harsh-named halt, that shields
> Workmen at dawn; swerving to solitude
> Of skies and scarecrows, haystacks, hares and pheasants,
> And the widening river's slow presence,
>
> Gathers to the surprise of a large town.

Highly vectored, assaying, emphatic, deliberate, the effect is of a
Yeats cast into another mould. However, when he writes or speaks
about the poet's role or occupation he tends to burst into fretful
disavowals of all that his great modernist predecessors seem to
postulate. 'Tradition', so important to Eliot and Pound, is now either
a museum or an incubus, like Yeats who causes you to expend your
talent in a waste of mimicry—'I have no belief in tradition or a
common myth-kitty or casual allusions in poems to other poems or
poets, which last I find unpleasantly like the talk of literary under-
strappers letting you see they know the right people.'[16] But surely
the Thomas Hardy who 'taught him to feel rather than to write', and
also taught him that he 'needn't jack himself up to a concept of
poetry that lay beyond his own life'[17] is equally a way in which
tradition may assert itself? Isn't it comparable with the kind of
encouragement Yeats got from the examples of Burns and Villon?
Again, though he may not believe in a 'myth-kitty', he certainly has
his 'mythologies', which do have more of Roland Barthes than Yeats
about them, whether they take the form of advertisement hoardings
or glamorous store clothing—he knows the hunger for 'transcen-
dence' that is the permanent impulse to myth.

Against the specifically audience-ignoring pronouncements of
Yeats, Pound and Eliot, Larkin also claims to be out to woo a
particular audience as a condition of his being able to make a poem at
all. This also belongs with his statement that he is out, in his poems,
to 'pickle' an experience—an experience which, we might say, he
and the audience already share, and which precedes or surrounds or
survives the poem which is 'about' it and serves it. The appeal to an
audience, which he hopes will have a certain congruence with the
audience for the poems of Sir John Betjeman, is thus simultaneously
a devaluing of the 'status' of the poem itself.

To the sharing of this experience any idea of a specially 'trained'
critical capacity is irrelevant, obfuscating nonsense. Poetic obscurity
itself he regards with suspicion as the dubious fruit of the institu-
tionalizing of the study of literature. Aggressively and reprehensibly
he invokes the idea of a 'pleasure-loving audience for whom the
dutiful mob that signs on every September is no substitute'.[18] (As he

[16] In D.J. Enright (ed.)'s *Poets of the 1950's* (Tokyo, 1955), p. 78.
[17] *Listener*, 25 July 1968, p. 111.
[18] Philip Larkin, 'The Pleasure Principle,' *Listen*, II (summer-autumn
1957), p. 28.

deliberately invokes 'pleasure' in a rather crude way and spares no pains to make his phrasing offensive we might remember Bentham's hedonic calculus and Mill's towering rebuke: 'Better Socrates dissatisfied than a pig satisfied.') That his 'position' drives him into revealing paradoxicality is shown by his complaint to Ian Hamilton about 'how low the level of critical understanding is; maybe the average reader can understand what I say, but the above-average often can't.' The late Merle Brown offers what might seem to be the only possible starting-point when he observes that the reader's 'discomfort with the poems, his not understanding them Larkin's way, coincides with his understanding them truthfully.'[19] In fact it is because of this strong sense that one does get of opposing possibilities in reading him that he ends by almost resembling what he most seems to wish to put behind him.

His apparent deference to an audience's requirements is actually a means to a very 'hegemonistic' relationship. Strategies in the poems themselves confirm this, for example the famous last stanza of 'An Arundel Tomb'. This is an exquisitely beautiful poem in which:

> The earl and countess lie in stone

unremarkably, the speaker claims, until:

> One sees, with a sharp tender shock,
> His hand withdrawn, holding her hand.

But in working up to his 'big finish' (which is how he sees it himself) he typically finesses with dutiful qualification, as if to guarantee his invulnerability and prevent by prior enactment any irrelevant intrusion of the reader's inconvenient responsiveness. Perhaps the poem is itself too marmoreal by half. Was he aware of Auden's embarrassment over his curiously similar 'big-finishing' line 'We must love one another or die'?

> Time has transfigured them into
> Untruth. The stone fidelity
> They hardly meant has come to be
> Their final blazon, and to prove
> Our almost-instinct almost true:
> What will survive of us is love.

[19] Merle Brown, *Double Lyric: Divisiveness and Communal Creativity in Recent English Poetry* (London, 1980), p. 84.

That the relationship with the reader is extremely 'hegemonistic' is also shown by the shows of doubt in another famous poem, 'Church Going', where, when the poet observes that he has 'no idea/ What this accoutred frowsty barn is worth' the sourly witty overplus of 'valuing' words is really blowing the gaff on his omniscient agnosticism. In general Larkin's words are enormously scrupulous, pondered, 'assaying' (in 'Here' the practice is close to becoming a tic). This habit seems to derive from Eliot, though Larkin has no instance as stultifyingly complex as:

> Only at nightfall, etherial rumours
> Revive for a moment a broken Coriolanus

from *The Waste Land*. But as a mode of perceiving, however close he might seem to be to a Hardy, whose work often figures the furtive 'voyeur' and the unobserved observer, his characteristic poems are far closer to Eliot, whose impotent 'consciousness' is Larkin's *donnée* and starting-point.

'The Whitsun Weddings', for example, which has the same reputation as the 'quintessential' Larkin poem as Eliot's *Waste Land* is supposedly his, is as regularly praised for its power as objected to on account of the dismissive or reductive terms it applies to its 'unconscious' denizens. Spender, for one, bridled at Eliot's early poetry— 'the psychology of his people is incredibly crude'. Larkin too, is vulnerable here partly because though the act of 'noticing' gives him his private 'epiphany', he refuses to 'defamiliarize':

> The fathers with broad belts under their suits
> And seamy foreheads; mothers loud and fat;
> An uncle shouting smut; and then the perms,
> The nylon gloves and jewellery-substitutes,
> The lemons, mauves and olive-ochres that
>
> Marked off the girls unreally from the rest.
>     Yes, from cafés
> And banquet halls up yards, and bunting-dressed
> Coach-party annexes, the wedding-days
> Were coming to an end.

Although the poet's overt appeal is to his celebration of, his 'standing by', 'his people' as in themselves they really are, in the strange way he does, it makes just as much sense to see them as being there for the sake of the poem rather than the other way round. It is part of the *don du poème*, in Mallarmé's phrase, that the greater their grossness, ordinariness, cultural dereliction, the greater the 'reach' of the poem that 'celebrates' them. By means transparently derived from Eliot's *Waste Land* he invests the 'pitiful modern instance' with positively anthropological 'reverberations', and, again pressing very close indeed to Eliot's method, invests a casual utterance with similar overtones:

> The women shared
> The secret like a happy funeral;
> While girls, gripping their handbags tighter, stared
> At a religious wounding . . .

> . . . Just long enough to settle hats and say
> *I nearly died*

which is true, if mannered—a ritual sense emerging from a 'scenario' as realistic as his friend Kingsley Amis's novels, with its Odeon, cooling tower and 'someone running up to bowl'. Yet the besetting introversion of the celebrant makes the poem stir intimations of solipsism which were such a prominent feature of *The Waste Land*:

> I thought of London spread out in the sun,
> Its postal districts packed like squares of wheat:

> There we were aimed. And as we raced across
>     Bright knots of rail
> Past standing Pullmans, walls of blackened moss
> Came close, and it was nearly done, this frail
> Travelling coincidence; and what it held
> Stood ready to be loosed with all the power
> That being changed can give. We slowed again,
> And as the tightened brakes took hold, there swelled
> A sense of falling, like an arrow-shower
> Sent out of sight, somewhere becoming rain.

But although the main point of reference seems to be the idea of fecundity—not to be taken too literally in terms of Tennyson's dismayed phrase about the 'torrent of babies'—there is, I feel, a 'convex' as well as a 'concave' reading in which the arrow shower is the impulse to the poem itself—the poem concludes by referring to its own genesis. Whether you call this ambivalence 'modernist' or not, it is very much at odds with Larkin's accounts of his own intentions and procedures. Another feature of his work that would surely be found dismayingly continental and arcane by the audience he imagines himself writing for is his 'ontological' awareness.

In last stanza of 'Here', for example, already quoted, it is 'Here' which is 'out of reach', which seems close to the Heideggerian paradox: *'Das Sein ist das Nächste. Doch die Nähe bleibt dem Menschen am weitesten'*. ('Being is the nearest to man. But this nearness remains furthest from him'.) Another poem which defines an act of turning away from the idea that changes in the social dispensation and socially created 'reality' can bring us 'degrees of freedom'—as Blake says, 'More! more! is the cry of the mistaken soul: less than all cannot satisfy man'—is 'High Windows'. Beginning as a sort of rancidly sardonic congratulation to the young on their sexual liberation (although I. A. Richards was already saying in the twenties that 'sex is the problem of our generation as religion was of the last'), the poem transcends the purely satirical 'Annus Mirabilis' when:

> immediately

> Rather than words comes the thought of high windows:
> The sun-comprehending glass,
> And beyond it, the deep blue air, that shows
> Nothing, and is nowhere, and is endless.

This could be read as nihilistic and in keeping with the death-wish expressed in 'Wants', but it has also the more positive resonance of what in 'The Old Fools' he calls 'the million-petalled flower/ Of being here'. But again, as in 'Here', we have, to use words Frank Lentricchia applies to Heidegger 'the conflict of existential and cultural *Dasein* and the consequent assignment of priority to the existential'.[20]

One could well imagine Larkin having a fine time with this quotation, which in the name of his audience he would refuse to understand and yet contrive to pour scorn on. Yet it is, finally, unfair to him to 'take' his poetry only on terms which he himself proposes. I attribute this to his desire to subvert 'modernism' and rehabilitate what Osborne's Jimmy Porter sarcastically calls 'something strong, something simple, something English'. 'Englishness' in Larkin is a

---

[20] The Heidegger quotation is from his *Brief über den Humanismus*; see Frank Lentricchia, *After the New Criticism* (London, 1980), p. 98.

means to perpetrate a form of cultural regression for which England has not always been notable. But by 'Larkin' here I mean only his pronouncements and attitudinizings. The poems themselves, which in another sense 'wrote "Larkin" ', are different. And unfortunately, if you combine precept and example, 'modernism' will in any case be found to contain too many of the qualities art has for your poems not to have some of them, if distinguished, as Larkin's are.

# VII

# The English Association and the Schools

## ALICIA PERCIVAL

We do not need to be continually looking at the origins of things—especially not at those of organizations, but the present time, as I hope may be agreed, seems appropriate to consider that of the English Association.

In our (i.e. not the Royal) Jubilee Year, 1956, an account was written (in Vol.9 of *Essays and Studies*) entitled *Half a Century of the English Association*. It is short but informative and was by that agreeable writer and good friend of the Association, Dr Arundel Esdaile. He says:

> ... The activities of our Association have been more widely concerned than entered the mind of its 'onlie begetter'. This was a Mr E.S. Valentine, Head of the English Department of Dundee High School and External Examiner in English in the Universities of Glasgow and St Andrews. On 15th January 1906, he wrote an identical letter to four leading English scholars ... in which he proposed 'a Society with many branches ... to keep its members in touch with what is freshest and best in this special department of educational work'.

He had to write other letters before he found anyone to help him to bring his idea into practical effect—and this helper was not 'a scholar'. (However, one is glad to know that Professor Bradley and the others to whom Valentine had written did join the Association when it was formed and played a useful part in it.) But the first to use the idea as the basis for a possible scheme was a Mr G.F.S. Coxhead, English master at Liverpool Collegiate School, and President of the I.A.A.M.[1] A preliminary meeting was held in Liverpool, followed by one in the University of London (then situated in South Kensington). The actual proposal, that the Association be founded, was moved by Dr (later Sir Philip) Hartog, who became Registrar of London University but who never ceased to work for the betterment of English Teaching in schools—the subject of his very forward-

[1]Incorporated Association of Assistant Masters

looking book, *The Writing of English*. He expressed the view that there was a great national work for an English Association to accomplish—which was probably going further than many of his audience would have followed. However, the Association was then formed and its purposes defined.

(The 'birthday', i.e. the day on which the Association came into being was 7 July 1906, less than six months after Valentine had written his original letters. Was the speed with which his idea became a reality a sign of the keenness of its founders, or does it merely reflect the ease with which in the 'good old days' such things could come about?)

As might be expected from the profession of its promoters, the educational aim of the society came first, but it was expanded thus:

> To afford opportunities for friendly intercourse and co-operation amongst all who love our literature and language and desire to spread a knowledge of them.

As Dr Esdaile put it: 'The double function of our Association was thus early defined.'

We need not, in order to trace the fulfilment of this first function, follow up the history of the Association as such (e.g. touch on the rise and decay of many of its branches). We have, as well as Dr Esdaile's, the account given by Dr Boas in the Association's fiftieth year, in *English*. Also, in 1977, Geoffrey Bellamy, of the University of Leicester, wrote *The History of the English Association, 1906–22* for his dissertation. Both of these have been consulted in the production of this account and should be acknowledged with thanks, though as explained, the special interest here lies in the carrying out by the Association of the primary aim of its founders. (Quotations, unless otherwise indicated, are from these accounts.)

However, though the origin of the English Association was in a specific sense scholastic, support fortunately came at once from scholars, eminent in their day—and still respected—such as Stopford Brooke, H.C. Beeching, W.P. Ker and F.S. Boas. It must have been the adherence of such as these which gave the new Association its standards and status. But to judge by the articles and correspondence (and it can be no surprise to find members of an English Association expressing themselves freely with criticisms and suggestions) it was accepted that the Association's activities were directed mainly to promoting the expansion of English in schools. It became recognized as an organization with knowledge about what went on (and what should be going on) in schools, from the point of view of the English teacher—now become the (specialist) teacher of English. But the English Association had also a wide outlook and well-considered principles which caused its views to be respected. Thus it was that when the Newbolt Committee was set up in 1919 to investigate English teaching, no fewer than nine out of the fourteen of which it consisted were members of the English Association and it was they who brought out in 1924 the very influential *Report on The Teaching of English* (Bellamy, p. 401).

Indeed, the Association was paying a great deal of attention in specific ways to the teaching of English in schools. Besides the production of articles and pamphlets, small conferences were organized for teachers (larger ones also, for members in general) where subjects like 'Oral English in Schools', 'Examinations', 'English throughout the School' were discussed. These meetings were sufficiently large for publishers to bring for display and purchase books suitable for introducing into schools. There were also the publications of the Association itself. The immensely popular *Poems of Today*, if not originally meant for schools, was certainly prepared with them in mind. The benefit here was mutual, as the English Association probably became known world-wide to more people through the anthology used in the schools (and even in examination papers) than by any other aspect of the Association at the time.

The Association used these specific ways to carry out its aims in schools but also used publications and propaganda to support the place of English in general and as a basis for all school subjects. These claims were put out on behalf of the teachers of English rather than addressed to them. It was the public, and particularly the educational authorities, who needed to be convinced. Belief in the expansion of English teaching was implicit in the aim originally formulated by Dr Boas: 'To unite and introduce to one another those who are interested in English Language and Literature . . . To uphold the standards of English writing and speech . . . To spread as widely as possible the knowledge and enjoyment of English literature . . .' To these Dr Boas had added a paragraph on putting these aims into practice: 'By organizing lectures, conferences and social functions, issuing a magazine and providing a Literary Advice Panel.' (Nearly all of these have been tried at different times with varying success; the last seems never to have been very acceptable.) As to the aims, which we have called 'general' and 'educational', Dr Boas as Hon.

Sec. seems to have held a satisfactory balance which enabled the Association to progress without too much internal discussion.

Perhaps this balance was kept well into the 1930s and it was after this that (as one sees in looking back) the Association became less and less concerned with the schools. It was only gradually—without its being intended or perhaps even perceived—that the more 'scholarly' interests, as found in the Universities, began to overshadow 'English in the Schools'. In 1942, Mr Nowell Smith, Headmaster of Sherborne, 'lamented the decline of the Association's educational activity and influence' (Bellamy, p. 267). There was, indeed, at a somewhat later period, a Schools Sub-Committee which might have actively promoted schemes or at least entered into a liaison with teachers' associations to discover in what way the Association could assist in the teaching of English in schools. Unfortunately this committee was of less use than it could have been owing to the temperament of the Chairman whose habit it was to veto every suggestion which was not in accord with the teaching of English as he had known and approved it. Eventually the Sub-Committee dissolved itself. (It is one of the major benefits of today's organization that a Schools Committee has again been appointed and is working well.)

However, other aspects of the Association were also growing in importance—reviewing, research, comment, and the general promotion of interest in the language and literature. The scholarly periodicals too, *The Year's Work in English Studies*, also *Essays and Studies*, were flourishing. The Association seems to have had a kind of revival after the Second World War. Perhaps I should confess to this as a personal experience; I had become a member, I think, in about 1938 but my first real interest in and appreciation of the Association was at a lively debate at a meeting arranged by Guy Boas, on a very scholastic subject—the place of set books in an examination syllabus. I was struck with the interest and spirit shown in the discussion and, when I began to go to more meetings, with the general liveliness of members at these proceedings. And clearly at that time the balance between the scholastic and general activities was accepted as satisfactory. But again, gradually and unintentionally, it seemed as if the more scholarly interests began to predominate. One must remember that among F.S. Boas's original statement of 'aim' was the phrase: 'to contribute to English letters, scholarship and research.' This was followed by the phrase: 'to discuss methods of teaching' and frankly, those who were guiding the policy of the Association found the former idea more interesting than the latter. That there would have been scope for the Association to become involved with schools on the teaching side is shown by the rise of other associations to engage on this work, notably the London Association of Teachers of English. It is a great satisfaction that a contact has now been made between this organization and the Association's Schools Committee.

Looking back, however, on this satisfactory period, one finds a number of different activities being easily and happily pursued— publications, lectures, conferences of different types (not forgetting the delightful residential ones at Christ's College, Cambridge) and including the Annual Lunches which follow the A.G.M. and the Presidential Address. The occasion is well-suited to the combination of 'listening folk and practical teachers'—as the Association's members were once described. It is perhaps not surprising that there has been a tendency to move from the educational side to what an early Headmaster called 'the more popular diffusion of literary culture'.

There was some reason for this. We have noted that often during the first two decades of this century at least, English had had to fight for its life to get any place at all in the school timetable. Its efforts were not helped by the belief that, if it had a place as a subject, it could be taught by an unqualified teacher on the staff, or that—'Any form-master can teach his form English.' (The equivalent in girls' schools was not so common. Whether English was better in girls' schools because of the higher place it was given in the curriculum or *vice versa* would be interesting to discuss, but not here.) But broadly speaking, the position had become quite different by the end of the 1920s. If, therefore, the primary motive for starting the Association was to ensure a reasonable place for English in the school, this had been achieved by about the 1930s. When the aim of an organization has been achieved, the organization must either find itself another aim, or fold up. The English Association had no intention of folding up—this would, to say nothing else, be a sad waste of all the effort that had gone into achieving the assured position it now held. Besides, there was so much it could do that was worth doing. Its work and the fellowship of its members could surely continue by accepting the more generalized of the aims propounded at the first meeting. That would allow almost any activity concerned with the language (and literature) that it felt capable of undertaking.

Clearly, none of this has been expressed in so many words, but looking back, one can see that it has come about. One great advantage of the Association is that it is capable of change, as a rule, to meet changing conditions and the needs of its members. For example, the need to change the office when the lease ran out has meant a change in communication with our members (to say nothing of a change in the office itself) who could visit us in South Kensington easily enough, or come to some function; that is hardly possible now.

Quite recently, however (to return to the theme of the Association's relations with the schools), there have been some important developments indicating that great attention is now being paid to the educational side of the Association's work. These are in a way developments of existing or former activities but they have been adjusted to the present, differing needs. I refer to the publication of the Association's *Grammar for Today*, to the Sixth Form Conferences, and to the Schools Committee.

There had been a suggestion as far back as 1954 that a new 'Outline of English Grammar' should be undertaken by the Association. Work was indeed done in this field by M. Alderton Pink, who, unfortunately, died in the following year and was greatly missed, and not only for his contributions on the educational side. But now, after some inevitable delay, this remarkable work by three members of the Association has been brought out—a contribution not to teachers and classes only but to all who are interested in a careful and enlightening study of the English Language.

Conferences innumerable there have been, sponsored by the English Association, to which have come teachers from every kind of school and educational background. They were no doubt helped by the discussion of common problems, and perhaps were enabled to see how something of their own experience could be carried over to the classroom. This would be an indirect approach to the children in the schools. These present conferences, as the name shows, are not for teachers but for sixth forms, and are geared specially to their examinations. The first of these took place in January 1973, in King's College, Strand, London. It was very well attended and these repeated occasions have increased in popularity; there are now far more applicants than places, although the Conference takes two days, the second being a repetition for different schools. (The entry is by schools, not individual pupils.) The pattern has been satisfactory enough not to require much changing; it includes a general lecture by some eminent speaker (and the main Hall is filled), then classes for the pupils and seminars for their teachers. (These last are optional; the pupils come with or without staff; the staff if present can do as they please about attending lectures or seminars.) For the sixth form classes, the set books for their examinations are the main topics of study. This eminently practical and scholarly exercise, which was new in form when it was started, is just the kind of activity appropriate to the English Association.

The Schools Committee formed in 1976 consists of members from an ever increasing number of schools, in different parts of the country. In organizing Conferences and other educational activities, it plays the part, in districts outside London, of the Association's Committee which arranges activities there. It is regarded as important to have an active country membership, and the schools in some ways take the place of the 'Branches' which in an earlier time represented the Association outside London. The work of the Schools Committee is very largely independent of the Central Office, though it is reported to the Executive Committee.

On this satisfactory note—that of real co-operation between the Association and the schools for which in part, at least, it was founded —we may close. It is not always realized for how long the English Association has existed, nor how many diverse activities it has, in the course of its existence, undertaken. But more and more one recognizes that the Association has its support from the interest taken in it by its members, whether individuals or groups such as the schools. (This is the last example to be given of the ability to change, to adapt itself to changing circumstances which is such a strength in the Association.) The pattern of its activities will change according to the demands made on it, as has been the case over these seventy years and more of its existence. May it long continue to change and yet to remain essentially the same!

# Notes on contributors

Elizabeth Maslen holds both London and Oxford degrees. She is now a lecturer in the English Department, Westfield College, London University, and has also lectured in Europe and the Far East. Her main academic interests are medieval and renaissance studies, and twentieth-century literature. She has published in *Archivum Linguisticum*, and a selection of her poems appears in *Treble Poets I* (1974).

Dr Betty Hill has taught at several British universities, most recently as Senior Lecturer at Leeds. She was an Assistant Editor of the *Dictionary of the Older Scottish Tongue*, and has published widely on medieval English texts and manuscripts. She is working on a facsimile edition of the seven texts of the *Conduct of Life* (formerly *Poema Morale*) and related studies.

Vivian Salmon, until recently Reader in English Language at Edinburgh University, is now an Honorary Fellow (Arts) of the University and is engaged on full-time research on the history of English in its social context. Her publications include studies in Old and Middle English language and literature, Elizabethan English, and the history of linguistic ideas.

Raymond Chapman is Professor of English Studies at the London School of Economics, University of London. He has written on Victorian literature, stylistics and the relationship between literature and theology. His books include *The Victorian Debate; Faith and Revolt: Studies in the Literature of the Oxford Movement; Linguistics and Literature; The Language of English Literature*. He is the Collector of *Essays and Studies* for 1984.

Roger Sharrock was Professor of English Language and Literature at King's College, London; he taught previously in the Universities of Southampton and Durham, holding the chair of English in the latter. His publications include *John Bunyan* (1954); *The Pilgrim's Progress* (1966); *The Pelican Book of English Prose* (1970); and the Oxford English Texts editions of *The Pilgrim's Progress* and *Grace Abounding*. A book on *The Novels of Graham Greene* is due for publication in 1983.

Dr Edward Neill, who teaches at Chelsea College, University of London and for the Open University, has published a number of articles in well-known periodicals, including *English* and the *Critical Quarterly*. He is also an inveterate book reviewer for journals including the *Times Literary* and the *Times Educational Supplements*.

Dr Alicia Percival read Classics and then English at St Hugh's College, Oxford. She has taught in schools and colleges both in England and overseas. At Trent Park Training College she was Vice-Principal. Her writings have been chiefly on biographical, educational and historical subjects.